westland ltd

Mandate: Will of the People

Vir Sanghvi is probably the best-known Indian journalist of his generation. He became editor of *Bombay magazine* at 22, making him the youngest editor in the history of Indian journalism. He went on to edit *Imprint* and *Sunday*, then India's largest-selling weekly newsmagazine. From 1999 to 2004, he was Editor of the *Hindustan Times* before being promoted to Editorial Director, a post he held till 2007, after which he continued at the paper as a columnist and advisor.

His television career has included several award-winning shows on the Star TV Network, NDTV and other channels. Most recently, he anchored two highly-regarded political series on NewsX, a channel he helped found.

He has a parallel career as India's leading food and travel writer and TV presenter. His many books include the best-selling *Men of Steel, Rude Food* (which won the Cointreau prize for Best Food Literature book in the world) and *Madhavrao Scindia, A Life.*

MANDATE: WILL OF THE PEOPLE

VIR SANGHVI

w

westland ltd

61, II Floor, Silverline Building, Alapakkam Main Road, Maduravoyal, Chennai 600095
93, I Floor, Sham Lal Road, Daryaganj, New Delhi 110002

First published by westland ltd 2015

10 9 8 7 6 5 4 3 2 1

ISBN: 978-93-84030-39-1

Typeset in: PrePSol Enterprises Pvt. Ltd.
Printed at: Thomson Press (India) Ltd.

For

Seema

Contents

Acknowledgements *ix*
Foreword *xi*
Introduction *xv*

Seeds of Dynasty 1

Evita 12

1984 34

Camelot 54

Mandal & Mandir 77

The Vajpayee Era 98

Cutting A Deal 115

Acknowledgements

This book was my wife, Seema Goswami's idea. Kartikeya Sharma of NewsX and I were discussing what kind of historical show to do when Seema had the idea of pegging it on the elections that had shaped India. Throughout the shoots, she travelled everywhere with me, finalized the scripts and helped with the edits. When the show turned into a book she was as involved. To her, I owe a huge debt of gratitude.

None of this would have been possible without Kartikeya Sharma, the rarest of news channel bosses. He was willing to invest in the months of research and travel required to collect all this information and yet, when we made the show, he never, ever interfered.

Many people at NewsX contributed to the enterprise. My core term was producer Ritika Srivastava and director of photography, Nishant Chandra. But many other played crucial roles. Bharat Raj, Pankaj Sharma and Saurav Saddi, who managed to persuade many people, who had remained silent for so long, to open up.

No one person could have compiled all the details required to piece events together. Fortunately I had two excellent researchers: Nitisha Tripathi and Divya Sethi.

Also at NewsX, Priya Sahgal, the channel's top political brain, helped enormously with advice.

My best critic has always been my son Raaj who watched every show and made penetrating criticisms. Many many thanks to him for helping his old man!

The only publisher I approached when the book was more or less ready, was Sudha Sadhanand of Westland who I have known since the early 1990s when we both did shows on the now defunct TVI. I called Sudha because I admired her political understanding and knew how important it is, for a book of this nature, to deal with an editor you respect. Also at Westland, thanks are due to Rahul Tanwar for the cover design.

And finally a huge thank you to Amish Tripathi. We knew each other only slightly and when Sudha suggested sending him a copy of the manuscript, I wondered why a bestselling author like him would waste his time on a little political book. I was not entirely wrong. He initially told Westland's CEO, Gautam Padmanabhan that he had no interest in writing forewords for books of this nature. To my delight he relented after he had read the manuscript and sent us a wonderful foreword without my ever having to call. Thanks Amish. You are a class act!

Vir Sanghvi

Foreword

The ancients believed that the perspective one has on time and phenomena is related to one's life-form. If you are a housefly (which lives for 15 to 30 days) and you are born during the Indian monsoon season, you would conclude that India is the land of unceasing rain. But if you're born a human being (which I suspect is the case), you would know better. Passage of time lends perspective to one's observations; perspective then leads to wisdom. And remember this: as the housefly is to a human being, a human being is to a nation.

A few years is a long period of time for a human being. But for a nation, it is nothing. To understand the real impact of changes in the national state of mind, one has to wait for at least a few decades. Having said that, I must confess it is entertaining to read the daily analysis (and predictions) of politics based on mercurial mood-swings of the people. With the advent of social media, it has now moved on from daily to minute-by-minute analysis.

If so inclined, I would recommend you go back and read articles from a few years or even a few months back; you'd be amazed by how off-target most observations and predictions were. I am not taking away the efforts exerted by analysts and journalists, though some of them undoubtedly can teach Don Quixote a thing or two about tilting at windmills. The problem is the absence of perspective, and the ability to extend into the past in order to make an extrapolation into the future; only time can offer this vision.

Herein lies the beauty of Vir's book. He gives one a sweeping vision of the mandates that the Indian people have blessed their politicians with over a fifty-year period. The benefit of time allows us to truly judge the impact of each election, going all the way back to the big one of 1971. The impact of some of these mandates is felt even today.

Since Vir has been in the thick of things for large parts of this period, and he certainly is one of the most perceptive thinkers of his generation, he has been able to bring out the key incidents in a succinct and easy-to-read manner. I completed this book in less than a couple of hours on a languid afternoon. I am old enough to have lived through much of what is written here. Other details and events, like the elections of 1971, were interesting to discover. The benefit of reading this compilation in just the right amount of detail is that it helps one gain some perspective on long-term progressive trends in the life of our nation.

So what did I learn? The mandates have reflected the will of the Indian people across various parameters: economic, social, religious et al. But since I am restricted by space (this is only a foreword; more's the pity!) I will dwell upon what I learnt on just one parameter: economic.

Firstly, with the benefit of hindsight, it is evident now that the hard, Left turn of the late 60s and early 70s was an economically unfortunate decision of the nation (remember, we voted for it!). Perhaps we were seduced by the fact that life was better in the 1950s when compared to the British Raj.

However, since the British Raj was economically one of the worst periods in Indian history since the dawn of time (we had near zero economic growth for more than a century), anything would have appeared better. And perhaps, experiencing the so-called success of planned growth and soft-socialism, the nation felt that it should double down on socialism. I spoke with my father after reading this book and he wryly recalled the tremendous hope that his generation had had from the 1971 election. They really believed that *"garibi"* would be *"hataoed"*. Of course, nothing of the sort transpired.

Eventually we were coerced by circumstances into shifting gears in 1991. And that hesitant shift towards capitalism, while not having been done with an ideological commitment, did put boosters on our economy. My generation benefitted to a large degree. We of course compare life today with the economic hardships that we faced as children in the 70s and 80s. Therefore, it is obvious that we would believe that economic Right-wing policies work. Has the nation doubled-down now towards more economic Right-wing thinking, (curiously tinged with Indian-style welfare), seeing the benefits that emerged over the last twenty years? Maybe that is a peek on one perspective of the 2014 elections.

Will our generation's hopes be realised? Will we be luckier than our parent's generation? Will we be able to transform into a developed country, banish poverty and take our rightful place in the comity of nations in our lifetime? We will know. In about twenty years. I am sure that Vir will write about that as well. I will be waiting.

In the meantime, I recommend that you read this book.

Amish

Introduction

This book began its life as a television series. I have long tired of the current trend in Indian news television where channels no longer feel obliged to report the news or to send correspondents out to cover stories. Instead, anchors assemble a dozen guests in a studio and on Outside Broadcast links and encourage them to disagree with each other — as angrily as possible. In the cacophony of raised voices and hurled insults that ensues, the subject under discussion is buried; facts are ignored and the viewer has learned nothing by the end of each show that he did not know before he reached for his remote.

I make no value judgements about this kind of TV programming. It seems to work; ratings are high. And it is the cheapest kind of TV to produce. All you need is a large desk and a few OB links. Moreover, you can go on the air at once, assembling a panel minutes before the show airs without having to worry about footage, scripts or even the facts.

But, as time has gone on, this type of TV has begun to bore me. It may get the viewers but there's very little satisfaction in being the ringmaster in some talk-circus. It is not that I long for the good old days when journalists went out and reported the news. It was more that I felt that we were missing out on the enormous possibilities that television offered. TV gives us the ability to examine our present, understand our past and assess our likely future. It lets us tell stories. And it allows us to record history for future generations. I wanted, desperately, to do a TV show that told a story; that took the many strands that constitute recent history and weaved them into a coherent whole.

This sounds noble in principle but in reality is difficult to do. Not only is it expensive and time consuming, it lacks the viewer appeal of a heated debate on the topic of the day. So which TV channel would be willing to shell out the money required to mount a series of this sort?

I was lucky to find Kartikeya Sharma of NewsX, a history buff, who was willing to assign the massive resources required for a project of this scale (cameramen, editors, producers, researchers, etc.) and to allow me the luxury of travelling all over India, from Thiruvananthapuram to Amritsar, to try and put the show together.

By the time I started to research the show, I had made the worrying discovery that whole generations of Indians had no real understanding of the political history of the last three decades. Partly, this was because they had been deliberately misinformed. Partly, it was because there was so little that was available to them in the form of popular history. And mostly, it was — dare I say this? — that we have become a society that prizes opinion over fact, argument over discussion, and a fuzzy view of a possible future over a clear understanding of the past.

A surprisingly large number of educated Indians under 30 have no real idea what the Emergency was, or even that there was a dangerous insurgency in Punjab during the 1980s.

When I finished the research and the interviews with primary sources and had ploughed through my own writings and interviews over the last three decades, I considered whether it was the time to put everything — including the stuff we had not been able to fit into the TV show — into a book. One of the attractions of doing the show (which was called Mandate With Destiny) was that unlike most news TV, it would not be dated. The episodes will withstand annual repeats and can be accessed on the net at any time.

But for you to get a sense of what happened in Indian politics from 1969 or so onwards, you would need to settle down for seven hours of TV viewing. It struck me then: what if I used all the material we had gathered and turned it into an easy-to-read, page-turning journey through modern Indian politics?

Though the book (like the show) is pegged on the general elections that shaped today's India (from 1971 onwards), the elections themselves really only serve to bookend each phase in Indian politics. This is not a book about voting trends or electoral turnouts. It is about the people, events and forces that contributed to the creation of the India we live in today.

It is not intended to be a work of serious history and so I have eschewed the pseudo-neutral tone of the historians. I write as a journalist and because so much of this is drawn from my own observations during that period, there are personal (and therefore, necessarily subjective) conclusions about leaders and their actions.

Nobody can pretend that one man's perspective is an accurate summary of recent events. I am sure there are things that went on behind the scenes that I missed. And I'm sure that many of the participants in the events I write about will dispute my analysis of them.

But, as far as possible, I've tried to be as fair as one can be without turning into a mealy-mouthed hypocrite or a mouthpiece for an antiseptic version of the flesh and blood people and battles that epitomised Indian politics over the last few decades.

My intention has been to produce a book that is well informed and gets its information as directly as possible from the principal players without trying to masquerade as a scholarly work. You should read it in one or two sittings and let the enormity of changes that have overcome India in recent decades seep slowly into your consciousness.

At the end of day, *Mandate: Will of the People* tells a story. It is an important story: how the world's largest democracy came of age. But it is still a story. So read the book for that story — and for how it has affected all our lives.

Chapter One

Seeds of Dynasty

1971 was India's first modern election. It was the election that changed the rules of Indian politics. And much of what we now regard as integral to our polity, first showed up in 1971.

That was the first election where personality and charisma made the difference between victory and defeat. It was the first election where the seeds of dynasty were sowed. And all of the things we now regard as part and parcel of Indian politics made their appearance in 1971: vote-bank politics, an appeal to the minorities and populism in the pursuit of votes.

The 1971 elections marked the emergence of Indira Gandhi and the birth of the party we know as the

Congress today. Oh yes, both had been around for years. But it was only in 1971 that they took the shape by which we know them today.

It is fashionable now to talk of Indira Gandhi as a dynast, as her father's chosen successor. In fact, there is very little evidence that Jawaharlal Nehru intended his daughter to succeed him. She lived in Teen Murti House with him but except for one stint as Congress President in the 1950s, never had any role in the government. When Nehru died, Lal Bahadur Shastri, his chosen successor became prime minister. And it was Shastri who brought Indira Gandhi into government, making her Information and Broadcasting Minister, hardly a major portfolio.

As time has gone on, there has been more and more disagreement over what Jawaharlal Nehru's plans for his daughter really were. Natwar Singh, who worked in Nehru's office and who knew Indira Gandhi well, says that while Nehru was always clear that his daughter would enter politics, he was not a dynast in the sense that he took it for granted that Indira Gandhi would succeed him one day. But Singh concedes that there is room for ambiguity on this score. Nehru rarely discussed his daughter's future with his staff, so it is hard for civil servants to be sure of what the Prime Minister really intended.

On the other hand, there are those who say that Nehru did have Indira Gandhi in mind as the eventual successor. Kuldip Nayar, the veteran journalist and Delhi insider, who later became Media Advisor to Lal Bahadur Shastri says that senior Congress leaders believed that Jawaharlal Nehru had a dynasty in mind.

Nayar recalls talking to K Kamaraj, the Tamil Nadu strongman who was then Congress President. Kamaraj told Nayar that when he discussed the succession with Nehru, the Prime Minister said, 'Indira, but not so soon.' Nehru then listed other options and one of them was Shastri.

What is clear however is that Shastri hated Mrs Gandhi. He included her in the cabinet as a concession to Nehru's memory but always believed that she was plotting to oust him and take the job herself. Shortly after Shastri took over as Prime Minister with additional charge of many ministries, he had a mild heart attack. Doctors advised him to cut down on his workload and to give up many of his departments. One of them was the major portfolio of External Affairs. During an informal discussion at the Prime Minister's Secretariat, he asked his aides for possible replacements.

Kuldip Nayar says he suggested Indira Gandhi's name.

Shastri rebuffed him at once. 'Nayar saab, you don't understand politics. She wants to be Prime Minister and you want me to give her the Foreign Ministry?'

And so, an uneasy truce persisted between the Prime Minister and his Information and Broadcasting Minister. Neither liked the other. But they had to learn to live together.

And that is how things might have remained. Except that in January 1966, Shastri died suddenly in Tashkent in the erstwhile Soviet Union where he had gone to sign a peace agreement with Ayub Khan of Pakistan on the conclusion of the 1965 Indo-Pak war.

Shastri's death threw the Congress into disarray. There was only one possible successor, Morarji Desai, the cranky, autocratic and self-proclaimed Gandhian who nobody could stand. So the old men and regional leaders who led the Congress in those days got together to find an alternative to Desai. They chose Indira Gandhi not because she was brilliant; quite the opposite. They chose her because she was pliable, a woman with no record of performance who would do their bidding. Ram Manohar Lohia, a veteran opposition leader and Socialist, dismissed Indira Gandhi in disgust as *gungi gudiya*—a dumb doll.

And indeed, for the first year of her prime ministership that is exactly what she was: faithfully following the instructions of her Congress bosses, of the old men the press called the Syndicate. In 1967, when India went to the polls, the Congress retained power but only just. It was badly mauled in the election and returned to office bruised and battered. Morarji Desai staked his claim to be prime minister once again and the Syndicate was only able to mollify him by making him Finance Minister and Deputy Prime Minister. His elevation meant a further decimation in Indira Gandhi's authority.

Morarji wasted no time in making it clear that he thought Indira Gandhi was a lightweight, a woman with little intellectual ability and no real competence to lead the government.

Nor was he shy about demonstrating his contempt. Natwar Singh remembers, 'Indiraji was not very good in economics and financial matters did not excite her. Morarji used to keep suggesting to her: "You don't know those things. I understand them better."'

And truth to tell, Mrs Gandhi was not an impressive prime minister in her first two years in office. Kuldip Nayar recalls that she was not even able to read her first few speeches properly. 'It was humiliating for me as an Indian,' he remembers. 'All the foreign correspondents were looking towards us and making fun of her.'

At what stage did the worm turn? When did Indira decide to become her own woman and take on the old men of the Syndicate? It is hard to say for sure but by 1969, with the Congress in decline and Morarji in an aggressive mood, she decided to take the battle to the door of the Congress bosses.

By now a kitchen cabinet had emerged at the Prime Minister's House comprising men like Dinesh Singh (who later became Foreign Minister) and the Left-leaning intellectual, Romesh Thapar. They became Indira Gandhi's brains trust.

But the key development was the departure of L K Jha from the Prime Minister's Secretariat and the arrival of P N Haksar.

Haksar had been Deputy High Commissioner at the Indian Mission in London when Mrs Gandhi recalled him to India in May 1967 and told him to take charge of her office. Friends and enemies alike agree that Haksar was one of the most brilliant men to have served in the Prime Minister's Secretariat.

He was part of a generation of Indian Leftists who deeply distrusted the United States, felt an ideological affinity with the Soviet bloc and had contempt for India's capitalists. Though he is rarely talked about these days because he was content to remain in the shadows, Haksar more than any other individual—except Indira Gandhi—determined the fortunes of the Indian State from 1967 to 1974. Had he continued in London as a diplomat and not returned to India to guide Indira Gandhi, history might have been very different.

It was Haksar's strategy that determined what Mrs Gandhi did next.

* * *

Any fool could see that the Congress was in terminal decline. Nobody seriously expected the party to win the next general election, due in 1972. So Mrs Gandhi probably decided that she had nothing to lose. And though she had never before demonstrated any love for Karl Marx, she now announced that she was a Socialist who would dismantle the Capitalist system, attack privilege and work for the poor. She attacked India's princes and took away their privy purses. She nationalised the country's largest banks. And she grew closer to the Communist parties.

The Syndicate was taken by surprise by this sudden lurch to the Left. It suspected that she was getting ready to challenge its authority. And the right opportunity came with the Presidential election of 1969.

The official Congress candidate was Neelam Sanjeeva Reddy, a fully paid-up member of the Syndicate and the Congress boss of Andhra Pradesh. But V V Giri, a veteran trade union leader who had served an undistinguished tenure as Vice President, decided to enter the fray as an independent candidate. Mrs Gandhi saw Giri's candidacy as a perfect opportunity to defeat Sanjeeva Reddy, her party's official candidate. She refused to openly support Reddy and then on the eve of the election, asked for a "conscience vote".

Natwar Singh believes that without Haksar's insistence on a fight to the finish, Mrs Gandhi would never have found the courage to take the Syndicate on. 'Initially, Mrs Gandhi had supported Sanjeeva Reddy,' says Natwar Singh. 'It was Haksar who made her change her mind. He told her, "You've got to take them on. You have to dig your heels in." And that's what she did.'

When the results were in, the Syndicate was humiliated. Reddy lost. And Giri won. Or put another way, the Syndicate lost. And Indira Gandhi won.

The Syndicate which still controlled the Congress organisation reacted with anger and outrage. The party officially expelled Indira Gandhi for anti-party activities. By all rights, as the Congress was the party in power and as it had expelled Indira Gandhi, the Prime Minister should have resigned.

But Mrs Gandhi was not a quitter. She refused to resign. Instead she split the Congress. Her branch did not have enough Members of Parliament or MPs to command a majority. But no matter, her new friends—the Communists—agreed to support her minority government from the outside.

So, as the Syndicate fretted and fumed, Indira Gandhi hung on to power.

But this was not a situation that could last. At some stage, her minority government, the first in India's history, would fall. So, in December 1970, she called a general election, one year ahead of schedule.

By all accounts, Indira Gandhi should have lost. The conventional wisdom was that elections were won or lost on the basis of party organisations. The Congress had won every election since Independence because it had the largest and best financial organisation of all the parties, with units in every single constituency. Then there was the arithmetic. The Syndicate-led Congress was now called the Congress (O) and it had presumably held on to at least half the old Congress' vote. The Congress (O) went into what was called "The Grand Alliance", joining up with other parties to field a single candidate against Mrs Gandhi's nominee. With organisation and arithmetic against her, it was hard to see how Indira Gandhi could win.

But 1971 was the election that proved that the importance of party organisation was over-rated. Indira Gandhi's candidates were younger, under-financed and not backed by grass roots workers. What they did have behind them however was the charisma of their leader. Indira Gandhi toured India extensively, addressing three or four meetings a day, flying from town to village by helicopter.

As a schoolboy, I attended one of her meetings in Rajasthan. She was not, I have to say, a very impressive speaker. Her voice was shrill and I thought the arguments were hackneyed. But the crowd felt differently. '*Woh kehte hain, Indira hatao,*' (They say, remove Indira), she said. '*Main kehti hoon, garibi hatao,*' (I say, remove poverty) she trilled. The applause was thunderous. And then, at the end, when she asked the crowd to repeat after her, 'Samajwaad Zindabad!' (Hail Socialism!), the roar was so loud I'm sure it could be heard for miles.

Even as a child, I could tell that something significant and important was happening. Indira Gandhi had captured the imagination of the Indian people. She had no party organisation. But she had charisma.

What I did not know then was that she also had a sound strategic vision. She had worked out that people were fed up of the Congress which had ruled India since Independence. They wanted a change. And what better change could there be than change with continuity. The alternative to the Congress had emerged from within the Congress itself.

We talk now of demographics and generational changes in Indian politics. And though nobody used those terms then, that was exactly what happened.

Since 1947, the same people had ruled India. This was a generation of freedom fighters—men who could always point to their role in the struggle for independence. By 1971, it was clear that they had failed to deliver. Nearly twenty-five years after Independence, India was still poor and backward. Many old-timers argued then that they had actually been better off in the days of the Raj. There was less poverty, the roads were cleaner, the cities were better planned and because there were fewer Indians there was more to go around.

The freedom fighters generation was seen as failures. They had lost one war to China in humiliating circumstances and a semi-victory over Pakistan in 1965 had done little to restore national pride.

India needed a new generation. It needed new ideas, new policies and new faces. Anyone who offered radical change was certain to appeal to the electorate. Haksar had told Mrs Gandhi that the best kind of change was the kind that empowered the people. And so she took many of the old edifices of the failing capitalist structure and nationalised them on behalf of the people: banks, coal mines, insurance companies etc. Just as she had stripped the princes of their privileges, she promised now to strip the old industrial barons and the political nawabs of their wealth and their influence.

These days we are skeptical of the State and of government. But in 1971, Indira Gandhi managed to identify the State with the people. It was not the government that was nationalising the banks, she said, it was the people of India who were taking them over so that the wealth could be distributed more equitably and not concentrated in the hands of the same industrial and business elite that had controlled the economy for decades.

We may laugh now at the naiveté of the idea that nationalisation of industries actually benefits anybody. But it is instructive how the themes that Mrs Gandhi introduced to Indian politics in 1977 are still dominant in our political discourse. She painted the Syndicate as being in the grips of crony capitalists—and that is an idea that every party from the Left to the Aam Aadmi Party (AAP) recycles again and again. She spoke of ending an era of privilege, of breaking up cosy cartels and of sharing the national wealth. The very same ideas were to re-appear in one form or the other in the 2014 election.

It is worth remembering that till 1971 nobody believed that charisma and populism could win elections. It was Indira Gandhi who demonstrated that they could.

There was more. Indira Gandhi recognised that the Muslims could be an important vote-bank. So she deliberately catered to their needs by focussing on issues such as the promotion of Urdu which she thought would win Muslim votes. Others have since followed her lead.

And then there were the roots of dynasty. When India rejects a political party that has ruled it for over twenty years and chooses an individual over everything else, it sends a powerful message. That message is: our future is in your hands. And when an individual gets such devotion from India's teeming millions, it is hard not to let the power go to your head and to believe that your own personality is more important than principles or ideology. It cannot be a co-incidence that within four years after this election, Indira Gandhi had more or less anointed her younger son as Crown Prince.

When the 1971 election gave Indira Gandhi a massive victory—she won 350 seats versus the Syndicate's 50 odd, many people believed that now that she was the upholder of the Congress legacy, she would rebuild and re-invent the party of her father and grandfather.

In fact, she did no such thing. The Congress withered away. The cult of her own personality flourished. And four years after this massive triumph for Indian democracy, Indira Gandhi went on to suspend democracy itself.

Chapter Two

Evita

In 1972, Indira Gandhi was at the height of her power. In the winter of 1971, the Indian army had defeated Pakistan, liberated its eastern part and helped create Bangladesh. The following year the Congress had won nine state elections by a huge majority. The opposition was in disarray. As the *Economist* magazine said, Indira Gandhi was not only Empress of India; she was also the only man in her cabinet.

So how did it all go so wrong? How did Indira Gandhi's popularity plummet so calamitously that she clung on to power only by suspending democracy, by censoring the press and by locking up the opposition? How did she lose her own seat? And then how did she make the most spectacular of comebacks? In short, how did Indira Gandhi make that journey to hell and back?

But the story of the 1977 election actually starts three years earlier, in 1974.

In 1973, after the Arab-Israeli War, the price of oil went up several times. The global economy tanked and massive and unprecedented inflation ravaged the economies of most countries.

In India, still struggling to banish poverty, the effects were felt most acutely. As prices rose and economic development slowed, the youth spilled out onto the streets to protest. Politicians became the objects of derision and their reputations have still not recovered. The new icons were the men who fought the system, of those who lived by their own rules, a trend that was reflected in Hindi cinema where the Angry Young Man replaced the romantic heroes of old.

If you were to pick the single worst year since Independence, then it would probably be 1974. You could argue that much of what had gone wrong was not Mrs Gandhi's fault. If the global economy tanks and inflation sweeps the world, then an underdeveloped country like India can hardly expect to be an exception to the trend.

But Indira Gandhi had a singular problem of her own: she had promised too much and delivered too little. At the 1971 general election and during the assembly poll of 1972, she had spoken of *"garibi hatao"*. But the *garib* or poor was even worse off in 1974 than he had been in 1971. None of her big ticket ideas—bank nationalisation, the takeover of the Public Distribution System (PDS), derecognising the maharajas etc., had delivered prosperity to India's poor.

And it wasn't just the poor who were dissatisfied and impatient. Within the Congress there were men like Chandrashekhar and Mohan Dharia who had led the fight against the Syndicate and believed that a new Socialist paradise was about to be created. When things went wrong, these Young Turks began to oppose Indira Gandhi just as violently as they had once opposed the Syndicate.

It is legitimate to ask how different things would have been if the Arab-Israeli War of 1973 had not led to the huge rise in oil prices and inflation had not spread across the world. Perhaps things would have been different. Perhaps Mrs Gandhi would have been able to deliver on at least some of her promises.

But history has little time for ifs and buts. And so, as the economy collapsed, Mrs Gandhi began to lose control of the instruments of governance.

* * *

As change spread across India, Indira Gandhi was taken by surprise. She was shocked when the people's movement against corruption took the form of street protests and annoyed when her father's old friend, Jayaprakash Narayan or JP emerged from retirement to become the spiritual leader of the protesters. By 1975, as the protests swept north India and Gujarat, Mrs Gandhi had an unexpected problem. In 1971, she had easily defeated Raj Narain, a clownish Socialist leader in the parliamentary constituency of Raibareli. When Narain had filed a petition accusing her of electoral malpractice, she had dismissed this as the complaint of a sore loser. And yet, as spring turned into summer, there were disconcerting rumours. Could it be, people speculated, that the Allahabad High Court might actually hold Indira Gandhi guilty of electoral offenses? Could it possibly overturn the results of the election?

The judgement, when it came in June, was worse than any of Mrs Gandhi's supporters had expected. It dismissed most of Raj Narain's complaints but it held that Yashpal Kapoor, one of Indira's campaign managers, had still been a government servant when he participated in the campaign. Further, Uttar Pradesh or UP government officials had helped erect stages for Mrs Gandhi's campaign meetings.

On these grounds alone, Justice Jagmohanlal Sinha of the Allahabad High Court, held her guilty of malpractice and declared her election null and void. Mrs Gandhi was given a few days to appeal to the Supreme Court, which she duly did. But there were those in her office who believed that Indira Gandhi was the victim of a conspiracy. What's more, they believed that this conspiracy had been hatched by some of her closest advisors. Among those who subscribed to this view was her trusted personal assistant, R K Dhawan. And perhaps, he persuaded Mrs Gandhi that this was indeed the case.

Dhawan was Indira Gandhi's closest aide. But in power terms, he was strictly second-tier. Mrs Gandhi's most important advisors were a group of Leftists and fellow travellers who had unfettered access to her. They included: Rajni Patel, a leading barrister who had once been a card-carrying Communist and was later the Congress boss of Bombay (now Mumbai), D K Barooah, a Congress leader from Assam who became national President of the party and most significantly, Siddhartha Shankar Ray.

Of this group, Ray was probably the most influential. He was not a Communist. In fact, he was fighting the Communists in West Bengal where he was Chief Minister. He had known Mrs Gandhi for years, called her by her first name, and was the man she turned to first for political advice.

This group had replaced P N Haksar who, though he still worked part-time at the Prime Minister's Secretariat, had retired and restricted himself to handling relations with the newly created state of Bangladesh. Mrs Gandhi had a new Secretary in her Secretariat, P N Dhar, a distinguished and well-respected economist. But Dhar was not a political person and often his advice was considered too principled and morally-elevated by Mrs Gandhi's new advisors.

According to Dhawan, Siddhartha Shankar Ray sent a handwritten note to Mrs Gandhi on 2 February 1975 stating that the situation was going out of control and something like an Emergency should be declared. He wanted her to prepare a list of dissidents, opposition leaders and to suspend several institutions of democracy. Indira Gandhi refused.

But then, says Dhawan, Ray and his friends began to show enormous interest in the Allahabad judgement. Till then the Prime Minister's Office (PMO), in common with the press, had treated the Raj Narain case as no more than a minor irritant. However, Dhawan began to get suspicious when he found that Ray and his friends seemed obsessed with the judgement.

According to Dhawan, a few days before the judgement, the then Law Minister H R Gokhale, who was close to Rajni Patel, Ray and the others, sent for him.

He found Ray, Barooah and Patel also present. They told him to make sure that Mrs Gandhi's lawyer should be present in the Allahabad High Court to receive a copy of the judgement so that it could be rushed to Delhi and an appeal filed in the Supreme Court.

Dhawan says he thought this was odd. He went back and told Mrs Gandhi about the meeting. 'I told her, "I suspect these people. They know what is in store for you." But she brushed me aside.'

Indira Gandhi told Dhawan that he was always needlessly suspicious of people and not to worry about the Allahabad case. But she remembered his doubts because, when the judgement was declared at 10 am on 12 June, the first person to call on her was Siddhartha Shankar Ray.

'We have lost,' he told her.

'Yes,' said Mrs Gandhi. 'But you probably knew about it in advance.'

Dhawan's theory—and it must be emphasised that he has no proof—is that Gokhale as Law Minister had discovered what the judgement was going to be. Once the judgement was announced, they expected that Mrs Gandhi would step down till the Supreme Court cleared her. And in the interim, Ray and the others would push for D K Barooah, the Congress President, as the interim prime minister.

We will never know if Dhawan's suspicions were valid. But once the judgement was declared, some note had to be taken of it.

There were two ways of looking at the judgement. There was Indira Gandhi's own view; she believed that the offences were relatively minor in nature. Also that she had appealed in the Supreme Court and it was bound to give her a stay. So, from her point of view, there was no crisis. But that's not how her critics saw it. The judgement came when her popularity was at an all-time low. For her detractors, this was a heaven-sent opportunity, a chance to rid India of Indira once and for all.

Naturally, the protesters went for broke—there were demonstrations all over India, a dharna (or peaceful demonstration) was announced and at a rally in Delhi, JP made his now infamous remark that members of the armed forces should not follow illegal orders. From JP's perspective this was fair enough. Nobody should follow illegal orders. But from Mrs Gandhi's point of view, he was asking the armed forces to mutiny.

In the face of growing opposition, Mrs Gandhi's options narrowed.

Should she step aside briefly till the Supreme Court stayed the Allahabad judgement? Should she cling on to office? There is still some controversy over her son Sanjay Gandhi's exact role. Did he really persuade her to impose an Emergency? Or was the Emergency really the idea of some of Mrs Gandhi's closest advisors?

What we do know for certain is that the architect of the Emergency proclamation was Siddhartha Shankar Ray. It was he who told Indira Gandhi that she should declare an Emergency. An Emergency gave government the right to effectively suspend civil liberties and put most of the institutions of democracy into suspended animation.

Nobody knows why Mrs Gandhi agreed to the Emergency. Her supporters say she believed that India was drifting into anarchy. Her critics say that she was always a dictator at heart, determined to hold on to power, even when she had no legitimacy.

Once again, we have Dhawan's eyewitness account of drama that preceded the proclamation of the Emergency. According to him, Siddhartha Shankar Ray went to see Fakhruddin Ali Ahmed, the then President of India and assured him that an Emergency could easily be promulgated under the constitution. Then he came to see Mrs Gandhi, told her that it was possible and sent her off to Rashtrapati Bhavan to meet Ahmed. Dhawan went with her but sat in an anteroom. At the end of their meeting, the President and Prime Minister called him in. Mrs Gandhi told Ahmed that Dhawan would return with a draft of the Emergency ordinance.

The ordinance itself was drafted by Siddhartha Shankar Ray. Mrs Gandhi asked Ray whether she was constitutionally obliged to call a cabinet meeting before sending the ordinance to Rashtrapati Bhavan. No need, said Ray. Even if the Prime Minister consults a single minister, it constitutes a cabinet decision. Mrs Gandhi accepted his advice in its entirety; even Brahmananda Reddy, the then Home Minister was not informed!

Dhawan took the ordinance to Rashtrapati Bhavan. The President signed it. And with a single stroke of his pen, Fakhruddin Ali Ahmed suspended the institutions of Indian democracy!

So who knew what Mrs Gandhi was planning? There were various groups already at work. Haksar, already only marginally involved with the Prime Minister's Secretariat, suggested a consensual approach. He drafted a statement affirming faith in Indira Gandhi's leadership. This was circulated among the cabinet, most of whose members willingly signed it. Haksar however was bitterly opposed to the Emergency.

Then there was the Sanjay factor.

In popular perception, Sanjay Gandhi is the villain of the piece. Apparently Mrs Gandhi would have resigned instantly but Sanjay forced her to stay in office and to declare the Emergency. It is true that Sanjay and ministers such as, Bansi Lal who had been cultivating him, were not in favour of Indira Gandhi following the high-minded course. And it is also true that Sanjay supported the Emergency. But it does not seem to have been his idea. He knew so little about the constitution of India that he had no clue that such a move was even possible.

The broad consensus seems to be that it was Ray's baby, from start to finish. As Mrs Gandhi's most important advisor, he thought that he would become the uncrowned king of India once democracy was suspended.

* * *

For most Indians, the consequences of the Emergency were unthinkable. On the night that the Emergency was declared, the authorities cut off electricity to newspaper offices on Delhi's Bahadur Shah Zafar Marg. From the very next day, editors were told to submit their articles for pre-censorship. Opposition leaders awoke to midnight knocks on their doors. They were arrested and locked up indefinitely. So were some journalists.

Among the first to be locked up was Kuldip Nayar. He is clear that he never believed that any Indian government would arrest one of the seniormost editors of *The Indian Express*. He says he was told by a friend, Nikhil Chakravartty, editor of the Left-leaning journal, *Mainstream* to be careful. 'He told me if you have any papers in your house, be careful because you are going to be raided,' Nayar remembers, 'and he knew the other side (Mrs Gandhi's regime) very well, so I listened to him.'

The next day, when the police arrived at Nayar's house, he was ready for them. 'You can search for anything,' he told them. Oh no, they said, this is not a raid. Here are the warrants. We are here to arrest you.

Nayar's arrest terrified the journalistic community. If India's most famous editor could be summarily arrested, then nobody was safe. Nayar recalls how his wife was ostracised. Nobody would even talk to her and relatives ignored her calls. Such was the atmosphere of fear.

Even Mrs Gandhi's own ministers were shocked by how quickly things had changed. Information and Broadcasting Minister Inder Kumar Gujral had been one of Mrs Gandhi's closest friends, but even he was dressed down by Sanjay. Many years after the event, I finally persuaded him to sit down and tell me what had really happened.

This is an excerpt from an interview I did with I K Gujral:

> There are many versions of the story of you and Sanjay Gandhi and you ceasing to be Information and Broadcasting Minister. What actually happened? Let's finally hear the true story from you.
>
> **I K Gujral: You see, well...Sanjay is gone.**
>
> But history is history. You must tell the truth.

I K Gujral: It sounds very uncharitable of me. You see one thing became very clear. As soon as we came out of the cabinet meeting, the transfer of power had taken place.

From Indira to Sanjay?

I K Gujral: From mother to the son. And he wanted me... as the cabinet meeting ended, he said, "I want to see the news bulletins."

You were I & B Minister.

I K Gujral: Radio. So I told him, "That cannot be done." News bulletins are made public only after broadcast. Prior to that even I'd never see them. Because that would be interference. And since I said no rather loudly, Mrs Gandhi heard it. And she came in. She didn't know what to say but she thought I was right. So she said, "No. No. We will deal with it later."

But my mind was made up. By chance, I had good luck, in retrospect. A telephone call came to me from the Prime Minister's House that I should come that day. I went at about 10.30-11. And the Prime Minister had left for office by then. And as I was coming out, Sanjay came over and he was in a very brisk mood...because one of the channels on All India Radio had not carried Mrs Gandhi's speech, which was normal practice. But he was rather brisk... but I told him. I had to tell him.

What did he say to you?

I K Gujral: You know, I hesitate because...again he is gone.

No, no. But we have heard so many versions. Let's hear the truth.

I K Gujral: He said, *"Dekhiye, aisa nahin chalega"* (Look, this can't go on).

Aisa nahin chalega? (This can't go on?)

I K Gujral: I said, look here, *jab tak main hoon, aisa hee chalega* (As long as I am here, this is how things will be). And you will learn how to be polite.

You said that?

I K Gujral: And you will learn how to behave with the seniors. And I owe no responsibility to you. I'm your mother's minister, not yours. And I walked out.

And then?

I K Gujral: That was over. That evening it was over. So the next morning I got the notification. I was ready to leave and relieved too. Because I told my wife that after what happened with Sanjay, now I won't have to resign. It will follow. It did follow. Anyhow. I regret it because that was the end of a chapter in my life.

I K Gujral and Indira Gandhi, old friends for decades, never reconciled.

* * *

Looking back, we often forget two distinct things about the Emergency. The first is that it marked the beginnings of the governmental promotion of dynasty. Upto that point, Sanjay Gandhi had been regarded only as Indira Gandhi's loutish son with no talent for anything other than fixing cars. Now, he suddenly became India's most important man. He took over the Youth Congress and began to be projected by State media and the censored press as the answer to all of India's problems. Chief Ministers bowed before him, helped him put on his shoes or shivered with fear in his presence.

Old Indira Gandhi loyalists like Siddhartha Shankar Ray, ironically the architect of Emergency, were suddenly out of favour because Sanjay didn't like them. The Left, long an ally and a supporter of Indira Gandhi, was dismissed. When asked why, Sanjay said, 'I don't like Commies.'

The conventional view of Sanjay Gandhi is that he was a deeply cynical, goonda-like figure who seized power once democracy had been suspended mainly because it was there for the taking. But those who knew him during that period paint a different picture.

They see him as a man with no interest in politics—upto that moment—who got dragged into the fray because he genuinely wanted to help his mother. But once he had stepped into politics, he was no different from any other politician who falls victim to the praises of *chamchas* or yes-men.

R K Dhawan, who was perceived to be close to Sanjay at that point says that he changed once he started touring the country. 'All the Chief Ministers started eulogising him and telling him "you are a great leader"', Dhawan recalls. Meetings were arranged in the states to which paid crowds were bused in. Sanjay who was really new to politics, did not understand how he was being manipulated by Congress chief ministers, all of whom had mastered the art of sycophancy.

'All these people—N D Tiwari, Bansi Lal, Giani Zail Singh, P C Sethi and others—they got hold of him and started praising and praising him,' recalls Dhawan. 'It went to his head. He began to believe that he was really popular all over the country. At one stage, he himself told me: "You know, I am drawing much bigger crowds than Mummy!" He believed that these were real crowds and he was such a hero of the masses.'

Sanjay now set about declaring his own objectives for India, grandly described as his own 5-point programme. (His mother had already announced her own 20-point programme.) Much of this was unexceptional (plant more trees—etc.) but it was his obsession with family planning that proved to be most dangerous as chief ministers opted for sterilisation as a quick-fix measure over a long-term education-and-birth-control strategy.

But even as Sanjay was engaging in his own megalomaniacal exercises, some positive things were happening. The economy, which had tanked following the oil price hike of 1973, was back on track.

Much of this was due to tight monetary policy controls which led to a drop in inflation rates. But a lot of it also had to do with better enforcement. Smugglers were arrested, hoarders were locked up, corruption went down because petty officials were now too frightened to take bribes and the public sector ran more efficiently.

As things began to go well, Sanjay and Bansi Lal approached Mrs Gandhi with a bold suggestion: she should amend the constitution. They did not just want a new amendment or two. They wanted the whole system restructured.

Says Dhawan, 'They told Mrs Gandhi that there should be a new Constituent Assembly.' The idea was to ditch Westminster democracy and switch to a version of the French system. Mrs Gandhi would be a French-style-directly elected President and Sanjay would be Prime Minister. 'But she turned all these suggestions down,' recalls Dhawan. 'She was happy with the present system.'

Then, in 1977, when it seemed like the Emergency would go on forever or even that the constitution would be rewritten, Mrs Gandhi surprised the world. She declared a general election, one year after it was due.

Why did she do it?

The first—and least honourable thing—to remember about the decision is that she did it not out of some desire to let the people speak but because she thought she was going to win. From her perspective, this was perfect. She would have five more years in office. And she would be hailed as a true democrat.

So the important question really is not the "why?" question but the "how?" question. How was she so misled?

According to R K Dhawan who was by her side during this period, she was so cut off from people that like Sanjay, she ended up believing what the sycophants told her. If they told her things were going well and if her rallies seemed jam-packed, well then, she had no way of knowing any better. The press was censored and everybody else was too scared to say anything remotely critical. So, like all dictators, she became a prisoner of what her *chamchas* told her. But also like all dictators, by this stage, Indira Gandhi had become a deeply suspicious woman. She wasn't content to hear praise. She wanted proof: hard facts and numbers.

In that era, before opinion polls took off in India, politicians relied on the Intelligence Bureau or the IB for estimates of likely election results. So Mrs Gandhi waited for IB's survey. And when IB assured her that she would win a massive victory, she gave the go-ahead for elections.

So, was IB wrong? Well, yes and no. According to Dhawan who is, admittedly, a conspiracy theorist, the IB report was rigged. He says P N Dhar, Secretary to the Prime Minister, who was opposed to the Emergency put pressure on S N Mathur, the Director of IB and on other officers to produce a report that predicted a Congress victory.

Given the prevailing mood, this was not difficult to do. Nobody wanted to be the intelligence official who told Indira and Sanjay that they were unpopular and that the country would vote them out of office. Far better to predict a Congress victory. If the Congress did win, the Gandhis would thank IB. And if the Congress lost, well then, it didn't really matter what the Gandhis thought anyway, did it?

Afterwards, Sanjay Gandhi told people that he had opposed the idea of calling elections. Kuldip Nayar met Sanjay Gandhi, when he was out of power, and asked, 'Why did you call the election?'

'I didn't,' Sanjay told him flatly. In his scheme of things, he explained, there would have been no election for thirty years.

Nayar was startled. So who called it? Sanjay gestured towards his mother who was standing some distance away. 'Ask her. She did it.'

And she did. But to be fair, she did it in the expectation that things would go her way and that she would once again be hailed as the great democratic empress of India, not some nasty woman who had let the lights go out on the world's largest democracy.

But almost everything went wrong for Indira Gandhi. First of all, the opposition leaders, once they were released from jail, agreed to sink their differences to form the Janata Party to take on the Congress. Secondly, family planning emerged as the key issue in north India. Sterilisation of the poor had been one of Sanjay's pet projects. He believed that India had too many poor people. So, if you stopped the poor from reproducing, you could easily solve the problem of poverty because there would be fewer poor people.

Though Sanjay did not advocate a campaign of forced sterilisation, that's what it turned into. Government officials were given sterilisation targets which could only be met if the poor were forcibly sterilised. In Haryana, Bansi Lal, the Chief Minister pursued this campaign with such ferocity that a disparaging election slogan went: "*Nasbandi ke teen dalal: Indira, Sanjay, Bansi Lal*" (The three brokers of sterilisation—Indira, Sanjay and Bansi Lal).

Thirdly, there was the collapse of the vote-bank coalition that had won the 1971 election for Indira Gandhi. The Muslims were hostile to the sterilisation campaign. And they had heard rumours that Sanjay did not share his mother's affection for India's minorities. Plus, the Harijan vote went with Babu Jagjivan Ram.

One of the seniormost members of the cabinet and leader of India's Harijans, Jagjivan Ram quit the Congress shortly after elections were declared. He was opposed to the Emergency, he said, and with a few other senior leaders, walked out to form a new party called the Congress for Democracy, the CFD as it came to be known, and quickly aligned with Janata Party.

By the time polling day came around, most people suspected that the Congress might just lose. Even so, the quantum of the defeat came as a shock. The Congress shrunk to its lowest total ever. It was wiped out in north India and in Raebareli. Raj Narain defeated Indira Gandhi, this time fair and square. The unthinkable had happened; the clown had beaten the queen.

Nobody had ever thought that the defeat would be so complete. But Mrs Gandhi finally showed some grace in adversity with a conciliatory speech announcing her resignation. The Emergency was lifted and Sanjay Gandhi announced that he was giving up politics.

Suddenly, India had its first non-Congress government. But even as Janata leaders gathered in Delhi in triumph, the problems had begun. Who would be the new prime minister? The strong man of the Janata Party was a rustic farmers' leader from Uttar Pradesh called Charan Singh who claimed the job. But then, Jagjivan Ram, whose defection had probably swung the election, also had a strong claim. Plus, Ram had the greater ministerial experience.

So the great democratic experiment that was the Janata government began with a lack of democracy.

JP and Acharya Kripalani said they would choose the next prime minister. They ruled out anybody from the Jan Sangh because it had the Right-wing Rashtriya Swayamsevak Sangh or RSS antecedents. They ruled out Charan Singh who was regarded as a difficult customer. But more significantly, they ruled out Jagjivan Ram, the leader of India's Harijans, the man whose defection had swung the election for the Janata Party. Jagjivan Ram announced that this was part of the traditional prejudice against Harijans. And who knows? Perhaps he was right.

In its very first week, the Janata Party decided to forget about democracy. Instead JP took informal soundings and decided that the eighty-two-year-old Morarji Desai, an old warhorse who had served as Home Minister and Deputy Prime Minister under Indira Gandhi, was the best compromise candidate. Nobody liked Morarji when he was in the Congress and nobody liked him now. Within weeks, India's new rulers were at each other's throats. Jagjivan Ram hated Charan Singh who hated the RSS which hated the Socialists. And, oh yes, everybody hated Morarji.

***

The new government made matters worse for itself by trying to prosecute Indira Gandhi. In the immediate aftermath of her defeat, Mrs Gandhi had seemed tired and relieved. Sanjay had announced that he was giving up politics and presumably returning to motor mechanics. The Congress then tried to recast itself as a non-Gandhi party.

The irony was that Mrs Gandhi's biggest critics outside of Janata were her old cronies. At the first meeting of the Congress Working Committee (CWC) after the defeat, Siddhartha Shankar Ray, the architect of the Emergency, turned on V C Shukla, who had been Mrs Gandhi's Information and Broadcasting Minister. How had he dared to become so arrogant? How had the Emergency government allowed men like Ray to be sidelined? Shukla mumbled that he was acting on Sanjay's orders.

The new Janata government set up a Commission of Inquiry under Justice J C Shah to look into the excesses committed during the Emergency. On the very first day, H K Gokhale appeared to depose against Mrs Gandhi. Then came all the others: Dr C Subramaniam, T A Pai, D P Chattopadhyaya and Siddhartha Ray. None of them had dared to speak out against the Emergency. Now they fell over each other in denouncing Indira Gandhi.

One day, Mrs Gandhi turned up at the Commission. Almost the first person she bumped into was Ray who had come to depose against her. The encounter was awkward but Siddhartha tried to make light of it.

'You are looking very fit these days,' he said to Indira.

'Oh yes,' she replied as cheerily. 'You are doing everything possible to keep me fit.'

As Charan Singh, the new Home Minister pursued Indira Gandhi with all the dexterity of Inspector Clouseau, Mrs Gandhi found that she had no choice but to remain in politics. One attempt to arrest her turned into a farce when the judge threw out the case saying that there was no evidence at all against her. Commissions of inquiry were routinely disrupted by Congress supporters and the essential goonda within Sanjay now came to the fore as the Youth Congress took to the streets.

While this drama was being enacted, Mrs Gandhi once again formed a new party which she called Congress (I) after herself. She got elected again to parliament and visited the sites of atrocities against Harijans and those on the margins of our society. She even made a triumphant visit to London where she loudly attacked the Janata government and found time to go and see a musical. Unmindful of the irony she chose *Evita*, whose theme must have resonated with her!

And as the internal battles continued within Janata Party, Mrs Gandhi had an idea. She sent emissaries to Charan Singh. Why doesn't he topple Morarji and split the party? He could then become prime minister with outside support from the Congress?

It is a measure of the moral degradation of the Janata Party that Charan Singh—who had tried to arrest Indira Gandhi and who had himself spent the Emergency in jail—eagerly jumped at the offer. He broke the Janata Party. Morarji Desai was forced to resign. And Charan Singh was sworn in as Prime Minister of India.

But Mrs Gandhi was not done yet. When the new Prime Minister arrived in parliament to seek a vote of confidence, he was told that Madam had changed her mind. And so, without ever having won the confidence of the House, Charan Singh resigned as Prime Minister. Janata Party was in tatters. Mrs Gandhi was delighted. And fresh elections were called.

By the end of 1979, educated Indians were in despair. The Janata Party experiment had messed up a historic opportunity. Mrs Gandhi and Sanjay weren't really apologetic about the Emergency. So what was the thoughtful voter to do?

It turned out that he didn't have to do anything. The tide had turned. Demonstrating the same fervour with which it had once thrown her out, the Indian electorate now voted Indira Gandhi back in with a comfortable overall majority. By her side, sneering menacingly was Sanjay Gandhi. As the Congress took office in 1980, it was as if 1977 had never happened. Indira Gandhi had finally got the electoral endorsement she had wanted. It had come three years too late. But by God, she'd got it.

Indira Gandhi was once more the Empress of India. But as she was soon to discover, this crown was made of thorns and the Empire itself was riven with dissent and divisiveness. Four years later the problems would cost her own life.

Chapter Three

1984

It is still not clear how history will remember the general election of 1984. We should remember it as the election that yielded the greatest mandate in Indian history. But I suspect that we will also remember the murder and mayhem that preceded that mandate. A Prime Minister of India was shot dead in her own house by her own bodyguards. Thousands of innocent Sikhs were massacred on the streets of Delhi. And the principle of dynastic succession, already much talked about, was finally given an electoral seal of approval.

The thing to note about the 1984 election is that if the events of history had not intervened then, far from getting the largest mandate ever, the Congress would probably have lost the election. But, in the end, it was

Indira Gandhi who lost her life and the Congress that won the election.

The Indira Gandhi who returned to power in 1980, having humiliated her old tormentors in the Janata Party, was not the triumphant Empress who had won the 1971 election. This time around she seemed old and tired, less willing to fight battles, more willing to surround herself with *chamchas* and completely dependent on Sanjay Gandhi, her delinquent younger son.

As most important Congress leaders had deserted her during her spell in the wilderness, she brought in unfamiliar names, men like P V Narasimha Rao, a rootless politician who had been a notoriously unsuccessful Chief Minister of Andhra Pradesh. Or R Venkataraman, a Tamil politician who was unknown at a national level. But her biggest mistake may have been the choice of Giani Zail Singh, a former Chief Minister of Punjab with no great reputation for competence as Home Minister.

Most appointments were, in any case, cleared first by Sanjay and Zail Singh publicly declared that Sanjay Gandhi was his *rehnuma* or mentor. Effective power passed from the Cabinet to the Prime Minister's personal staff and R K Dhawan, Mrs Gandhi's trusted personal assistant, one of India's most powerful men, more important certainly than any cabinet minister.

But barely had the new regime settled in when, in a matter of months, tragedy struck. Sanjay Gandhi was known to be an enthusiastic if reckless pilot. Most mornings he would head to Safdarjung Airport and go for a joy ride in a Pitts Stunt aircraft gifted to him by the NRI millionaire, Swraj Paul. One particular morning, Sanjay lost control of his plane and it came crashing down in Willingdon Crescent, bang in the heart of governmental Delhi. Both Sanjay and his co-pilot were killed instantly.

The episode was tragic, but not surprising. R K Dhawan remembers going flying with Sanjay. He was shocked to see the Pitts Stunt plane. It had no roof, looked like a toy and to start it, you had to pull a string as you would with a generator. Sanjay tried so many acrobatics in the air that Dhawan was terrified throughout the flight.

Finally, he recalls, Sanjay landed the plane on the tarmac at Safdarjung Airport. But just as Dhawan had begun to breathe easy, Sanjay took off again for more acrobatics. When the two men—a nonchalant Sanjay and a shaken Dhawan—returned to the Prime Minister's house, they were greeted by Maneka, Sanjay's wife, who said acerbically to Sanjay. 'So you have come back alive.'

Dhawan went to see Mrs Gandhi. He told her that Sanjay was risking his life on foolish aerial acrobatics everyday. 'Madam, you have to be strict and restrain him,' Dhawan told her. We will never know whether she took his advice and spoke to Sanjay or she ignored Dhawan's warning. But her principal aide's fears were soon to be proved tragically prescient.

No parent should have to witness the gruesome death of one of their children. But for Indira Gandhi, the tragedy was more than just personal. Sanjay was the effective—if unofficial—Deputy Prime Minister. On every subject, with the possible exception of foreign affairs, his was the last word. Now, with his mother in a state of shock, the regime had lost its most important man.

Indira Gandhi took months to recover from Sanjay's death. And when she did return to a semblance of normality, it was only by pushing her older son, Rajiv to take Sanjay's place. Rajiv was aggressively non-political. His wife Sonia hated politics and vigorously opposed any move to draft him into politics. So, at first, Rajiv said no. He would stick to being a pilot for Indian Airlines.

But even that was not acceptable to Indira Gandhi. She had lost one son in an aeroplane crash. She was not going to allow the other to continue as a pilot. Eventually when his mother's pressure got too much, Rajiv Gandhi gave in and took the plunge, joining politics and becoming a General Secretary of the Congress. At the time people thought this was a bit odd. What did Mrs Gandhi's demand that one son replace the other say about the Congress? Was it her view that the party becomes a family-run private company? Perhaps it was. This was a new Congress, a party she had created herself during her spell in the wilderness, one she called Congress (I) after herself. From her perspective, yes, it was a family business.

But this also depended on how you defined family. Maneka, Sanjay's young widow, believed that she should succeed Sanjay. She was sharp, ambitious, political and eager to enter the family business. But no matter how hard she tried, Mrs Gandhi refused to let her replace Sanjay in the party. Eventually, in a soap opera that had Delhi riveted, Maneka stormed out of the Prime Minister's house, called her mother-in-law names and founded her own political party named after Sanjay.

While the Gandhi household was in turmoil, fires were breaking out all over India. First it was Assam.

A movement against outsiders, from Bangladesh and elsewhere, led by student leaders paralysed the state government and wrecked law and order. Even as the government coped with Assam, Punjab burst into flames. Much of this was the Congress' own doing. During the Janata Party regime, Zail Singh had persuaded Sanjay that the best hope for the Congress in Punjab lay in breaking the Akali Dal's hold on the gurudwaras. Zail Singh and other Congressmen promoted a radical and fiery preacher called Jarnail Singh Bhindranwale as a rival to the established Sikh leadership.

But while the Akalis and their allies in the gurudwaras were non-violent, Bhindranwale's followers operated through murder. And soon their rhetoric turned. They became not just anti-Congress but also anti-Hindu. Many Sikhs suddenly began claiming that they were a persecuted minority in India. A few demanded their own country to be called Khalistan. The thugs who had first flocked to Bhindranwale to bump off his political rivals now claimed to be fighting for the Sikh nation. As militancy spread throughout Punjab, so did the communal divide.

Sikh militants targeted prominent and influential Hindus and shot them dead. Sometimes they would stop buses, separate the Sikh passengers from the Hindus and then shoot all the Hindus dead. Through it all, Mrs Gandhi dithered. She depended on back-channel talks with the Akalis who were as worried by the rise of Bhindranwale's militant brigade as anybody else but were forced to take an anti-Delhi position in public. Even emissaries were sent to Bhindranwale but he said one thing one day and another thing the next.

Matters were not helped by the breakdown of the state administration. The Congress Chief Minister of Punjab, Darbara Singh blamed Zail Singh, his old political rival who, he said, was not only encouraging the militants but was also sabotaging the secret talks with the Akalis. But Mrs Gandhi liked Zail Singh. She had made him India's first Sikh President at which, Zail Singh had told an interviewer that he was so obedient to his leader that he would do whatever she asked. If she asked him to pick up a broom and sweep the floor, he would! Except that Indira Gandhi did not make Zail Singh a sweeper. She made him President of the world's largest republic.

By 1983 it was clear that Bhindranwale had to be stopped. The Punjab police were too scared of reprisals against their families to act against the militants and therefore needed some sort of Central intervention. The problem was that Bhindranwale and his gang of armed militants occupied a guest house at the edge of the Golden Temple complex. And Mrs Gandhi was reluctant to conduct a military operation anywhere near Sikhism's holiest shrine.

Indira Gandhi had missed many opportunities to stop Bhindranwale. In 1983, a Punjab police DIG called A S Atwal visited the Golden Temple. A militant shot him dead in cold blood and coolly sauntered off. Not only did nobody dare stop the killer but Atwal's body remained at the spot where he had been shot for several hours afterwards because no one had the guts to move it.

If Indira Gandhi had sent security personnel into the Golden Temple at that stage to apprehend the killer and to break up the murderous machine that the militants had created, moderate Sikhs would have supported the move. But Indira Gandhi hesitated and the opportunity was allowed to pass.

Satish Jacob who covered the Punjab militancy for the BBC remembers that incident well. 'It was a shock for everyone because no one had imagined a thing like that. Atwal was coming out of the Golden Temple with prasad in his hands and they shot him on the steps. The shocking thing was that though he was the seniormost police officer in Amritsar at the time, nobody had the guts to do anything. His body just lay there for 24 hours. Eventually the District Magistrate called Bhindranwale and pleaded with him and finally Bhindranwale allowed the police to come and collect the body.'

Jacob shares the view that they should have taken action against Bhindranwale in the aftermath of Atwal's murder. 'At that time,' he says, 'Bhindranwale was not that powerful. He was in a rest house called Guru Nanak Niwas which was not officially part of the Golden Temple. And he did not have a full team at the time. So they could easily have got him. But they didn't. Perhaps it was because, at that time, Giani Zail Singh was the Home Minister.'

By 1984, the situation in Punjab had swung dangerously out of control. After Atwal's murder, no policemen would act against the militants.Trucks laden with sophisticated weaponry were allowed into the Golden Temple because no cop had the courage to stop the militants from fortifying their base within the temple. For a full year, the government considered a commando operation to flush out the militants but each time, the idea was abandoned as being unfeasible.

Finally, in June 1984, the intelligence agencies reported to Indira Gandhi that the militants, with Pakistan's assistance, were ready to declare an independent state of Khalistan from inside the temple. This set off a panic in Delhi. The army chief was summoned and told to clear the temple of the militants. In retrospect, this was a crazy decision. The Indian army had no previous experience of fighting in built-up areas packed with civilians. Nor were the generals given enough time to prepare. They were told to clear the temple within a week.

But if Mrs Gandhi was wrong to send the army in, then the army itself was as much to blame. Its generals displayed a foolish overconfidence, bragging that the operation would be easy to execute and promising her that it would all be over in a few hours.

Nobody had told the generals that the day they chose for the operation—6 June was holy for Sikhs and that the temple would be filled with innocent pilgrims. Bhindranwale knew the military was approaching, so he shifted his base to the Akal Takht within the Golden Temple, and asked one of his aides, a cashiered Indian army general called Shabeg Singh to plan the defences. Shabeg turned the Akal Takht into a fortress.

When the army went in, its soldiers walked into an ambush as militants opened fire and cut down dozens of men. As the army operation floundered, desperation set in. The generals called for tanks and eventually defeated the militants by flattening the Akal Takht, damaging the Harmandir Sahib and killing many innocent pilgrims who were caught in the crossfire. Three days later, Bhindranwale was dead but even moderate Sikhs were outraged by the scale of the destruction. Sikh soldiers in the Indian army mutinied and the eminent Sikh writer, Khushwant Singh, a fierce critic of Bhindranwale, returned his Padma Bhushan in protest.

Could the fiasco been avoided? Satish Jacob who was in Amritsar during Operation Blue Star thinks that the Indian army's overconfidence led to the deaths of many of its own soldiers and of innocent pilgrims. 'They thought it was going to be a piece of cake. They didn't think it would take more than a day. There was no real planning, nothing. They were caught completely by surprise and by the end, they were so desperate that they brought tanks. Can you imagine that? Tanks inside the Golden Temple! It was a real mess.'

* * *

Even as the Punjab fiasco was unfolding, there were signs that the Congress was losing its grip over the country. In Andhra Pradesh, a new party launched by an actor called N T Rama Rao swept the polls, throwing out the Congress. In Karnataka, the Janata Party, consisting of remnants of the old 1977 grouping pulled off a coup by defeating the Congress and a charismatic chief minister called R K Hegde was installed. By-elections told the same story. Of the thirty by-elections to the Lok Sabha held during this period, the Congress lost most.

By now, the opposition was coming around to the view that the Indira-era was finally ending. Chandrashekhar, who had been the President of the Janata Party during its short-lived period in office from 1977-79 emerged as the prime minister-in-waiting. He went on a long, almost Gandhian, padayatra around India and presented his simple, unpretentious style as an alternative to Indira Gandhi's imperial arrogance. Sensing victory, the opposition organised conclaves all over India building up a national front to oppose the Congress in the general elections that were due in the winter of 1984-85.

Oddly enough, Indira Gandhi was not that worried by the spectre of electoral defeat. Those who knew her well say that something had changed within her after Operation Blue Star. She had a premonition that her life was in danger and began to make plans for what should happen in the event of her death. Her daughter-in-law, Sonia Gandhi told me years later that Mrs Gandhi had written out detailed instructions for each member of her family, even down to the manner in which her ashes would be disposed of.

But despite this threat, she did nothing in particular to ensure her own security. Her advisors removed Sikh policemen from her close protection detail. She noticed that they were missing and asked for them to be re-instated. Even Rajiv Gandhi noticed that a young, Delhi police constable seemed particularly sullen and requested that he be shifted to another part of the Prime Minister's house where he would not have such close access to Mrs Gandhi. But Indira would have none of it. No Sikh would be moved, she decreed.

On the morning of 31 October 1984, Indira Gandhi was walking from one part of the Prime Minister's house complex to another. She was due to shoot a TV interview with the British actor, Peter Ustinov. As she crossed over to the area where Ustinov and his crew were waiting, a Delhi police sub-inspector called Beant Singh who had recently been re-instated as part of PM's security detail pulled his revolver out of its holster and shot her at point-blank range. Then, the very same sullen police constable Rajiv Gandhi had been concerned about, sprayed her body with more bullets from his sten gun.

R K Dhawan was an eyewitness to the assassination. He went to see her just before she left for the interview. Mrs Gandhi was having her hair done and was preparing for having TV make-up applied. Outwardly, at least, it seemed like any other day. Mrs Gandhi told Dhawan that a foreign guest was coming for dinner but that the dinner clashed with the arrival of Giani Zail Singh from a foreign trip. Could Dhawan speak to the President's party and check if he could advance his arrival because she wanted to go to the airport to receive him?

Dhawan went back to his office to contact the President's aides when he was informed that the Prime Minister's household staff wanted the interview to be delayed. The previous day was the festival of Diwali and the lawn was littered with the debris of fire crackers which they wanted cleared before the Prime Minister walked across the lawn.

But Mrs Gandhi was a stickler for time and once her make-up was done, she sent for Dhawan and said, 'Let's go, anyway.' As they walked towards the spot where Ustinov's crew had set up the shoot, she saw a waiter going towards the TV unit with cups of tea. Meticulous to the last detail, she stopped him. 'These are the wrong cups,' she told him, 'Go back and get the right ones.'

They walked to the gate that divided the official part of the Prime Minister's house from the private residence when Beant Singh pulled out his gun and opened fire. Soon another policeman joined in. Dhawan stood rooted to the spot, shocked at what was happening.

Sonia Gandhi was in her room. She had met her mother-in-law briefly in the morning and planned to see her again after the interview. 'I heard some noises,' she remembers, 'which sounded a lot like Diwali *patakhas* (fire crackers). Diwali had just gone by. And then I heard my children's nanny screaming. And I knew at once that something terrible had happened.'

As Mrs Gandhi collapsed in a bloody heap, pandemonium broke out. The two assassins dropped their weapons and surrendered. 'We have done what we had to,' Beant Singh told jawans from the Indo-Tibetan Border Force (ITBP), who were also charged with providing security at Prime Minister's house. 'Now you do what you have to.' The second assassin, who turned out to be a young constable called Satwant Singh said nothing but offered no resistance. The ITBP jawans took the two men into custody and led them to their barricade. Nobody is quite sure what happened next but the jawans, apparently in a fit of rage, shot and killed Beant Singh. Satwant was shot as well but remained alive.

An elaborate security protocol had been worked out for such eventualities, such as an assassination. An ambulance was supposed to be on permanent stand by at Prime Minister's house. But everything failed that day. Not only were the assassins shot but the ambulance driver could not be found. He had, it was later revealed, stepped out for a cup of chai. Sonia Gandhi heard the shots and ran out into the lawn where her mother-in-law lay dying. 'Mummy! Oh my God, Mummy!' she screamed as she saw the blood ebbing out of Indira Gandhi's body. Sonia commandeered a white governmental Ambassador, put Mrs Gandhi's body in the back seat and sat with her, cradling her head, in her lap. The Ambassador sped to the All India Institute of Medical Sciences or AIIMS.

Even then, though the life of the Prime Minister of India was at stake, the typical governmental indifference and inefficiency were evident. Dhawan had told the staff at the Prime Minister's house to immediately call AIIMS to say that they were on their way. But when they arrived, there was no medical team waiting for them. They reversed the car, sped to the Emergency section, pushed aside the crowds of patients who were already waiting, and carried Mrs Gandhi into the hospital.

Slowly, the doctors began assembling to examine the fallen Prime Minister. And as panic spread, an operating theatre was prepared.

Rajiv Gandhi was in West Bengal when he heard that his mother had been shot. So was Pranab Mukherjee, then Finance Minister (now the President of India) and technically number two in the cabinet. They boarded a special Indian Airlines flight and rushed to Delhi. When they were halfway to the capital, Rajiv went into the cockpit and spoke to the controllers on the ground. They had a message for him. Despite the best efforts by doctors, Indira Gandhi had died. There had been too many bullets and she had lost too much blood.

Eyewitnesses say that when Rajiv emerged from the cockpit, he looked shattered but struggled to maintain his composure. 'She is no more,' he announced. Pranab Mukherjee was the first to react. He broke down and began crying loudly. Others also began to weep. Only Rajiv refused to let his emotions get the better of him.

Meanwhile, back in Delhi, crowds had begun to gather outside AIIMS as news of Mrs Gandhi's death spread. Within an hour, the mood turned ugly. President Zail Singh had just returned from a trip abroad and drove directly to AIIMS. His motorcade was stoned. If this was how the President of India was treated by the Delhi mob, then could ordinary Sikhs expect better. By the evening, fanciful and unsubstantiated stories that Sikhs were bursting crackers and distributing sweets to celebrate Indira Gandhi's assassination had begun to do the rounds.

Initially, it was believed that the Congress would opt for an elderly leader to take over as acting Prime Minister just as the veteran freedom fighter, Gulzarilal Nanda had done in the aftermath of Jawaharlal Nehru's death and later Lal Bahadur Shastri's demise. Later the parliamentary party would meet and formally elect Rajiv Gandhi as the new Prime Minister.

In fact, Zail Singh swore Rajiv Gandhi in as his mother's successor right away. One view is that the President, aware of his own dodgy role during the Punjab militancy and scared of the public anger that had led the mob to stone his car, simply did what the then Congress bosses, such as Arun Nehru instructed him to. A more plausible version is the one Zail Singh himself told me. He said that he too had been told by Mrs Gandhi that she might be assassinated. If that happened, she told him, he was to swear Rajiv immediately.

But the strongest objection to Rajiv Gandhi's accession did not come from an opposition worried about a dynastic transition. It came from Sonia Gandhi, his wife. P C Alexander, who had been Principal Secretary to Indira Gandhi walked into a room at AIIMS to find Rajiv hugging Sonia.

'Don't do it. Please don't take the job,' she told him. 'I have to do it. It will be all right,' he responded. Years later I asked Sonia Gandhi about Alexander's version of the incident. She confirmed every detail. 'Yes. That is exactly what happened. I was in a terrible state. I did not want my husband to become Prime Minister. I was literally begging him not to accept the post. And I told him I did not want him to do it because they would kill him. And my husband said, "I will be killed in any case."'

And so at forty-six, having been in politics for only four years and never having held any governmental office, Rajiv Gandhi became India's youngest ever Prime Minister even as doctors struggled to patch up his mother's body so that it would look presentable at her funeral.

What followed next was even more shameful and shocking than the assassination of India's Prime Minister by her own bodyguards. Mobs began to roam the streets looking for innocent Sikhs on whom they could take revenge for Mrs Gandhi's murder. Some of the violence must have been random. It takes only a flickering spark to set off a communal conflagration in India when tempers are running high.

But there is no doubt that much of the mayhem was organised. Too many eyewitnesses saw local Congress leaders at the heads of these mobs for all of these stories to be untrue. Nor was the bulk of the violence directed at burly Jat Sikhs who were likely to fight back. Instead the mobs went to resettlement colonies and picked on poor, slightly-built Mazhabi Sikhs who were less able to defend themselves. The stories of the violence of that era haunt anybody who lived through those massacres. In some cases, mobs placed two or three tyres around the bodies of their victims and then set fire to them, often in front of their wives and children.

And nobody bothered to help the poor victims in the resettlement colonies. The police force disappeared from the streets of Delhi. One conspiracy theory has it that the cops were told to let Delhi burn. What is more likely is that the force, already in shock and disgrace after two of its members assassinated the prime minister, saw that it had nothing to gain from risking the lives of its men by trying to stop the violence.

The administration was paralysed. The then Lt. Governor came under such sustained attack for this ineptitude that they had to sack him. P V Narasimha Rao was the Home Minister and he simply refused to get involved. Many years later when Chandrashekhar was Prime Minister, he told me a story about that period. A Sikh friend of his son's felt insecure. So Chandrashekhar's family told him to move in with them. But the boy was worried about the rest of his family. Chandrashekhar called Narasimha Rao and asked if he could offer them some protection. Oh no, said Rao, we can't offer protection to anyone. 'And anyway, Chandrashekharji, you should not ask that Sikh boy to stay in your house. It's too dangerous. Suppose a mob finds out you are harbouring a Sikh and comes and attacks your house!'

That was how the Home Minister of India protected Sikhs.

Ved Marwah one of India's most respected police officers was later asked by Rajiv Gandhi to conduct an inquiry into the failures of the police force during the riots. Marwah checked the records of the Police Control Room and found that calls came in every few minutes from affected parts of the city. The Control Room passed on the messages to police stations in these localities. But says Marwah, when he checked the records of the police stations he found that either the police officers did not go out to attend to those distress calls or that if they did, they kept no record.

Further Marwah discovered that the violence against the Sikhs was not of the sort usually associated with communal clashes. 'In many cases, they put tyres around the bodies of Sikhs and burnt them alive. The Sikhs took an hour to die. This kind of cruelty is not the handiwork of mobs angered by the assassination. This was the work of hard-core criminals,' he says.

So who mobilised these hard-core criminals? And who was so influential that the police refused to interfere when these criminals went about their savagery?

Marwah suggests that the answer is obvious. It was local politicians.

The Congress would say later that the murder, mayhem and chaos were partly a function of the suddenness of Mrs Gandhi's assassination. Rajiv took a day or two to settle down in office while simultaneously mourning his mother. He did not expect the home minister to abdicate all responsibility or the Delhi police to simply run away.

As soon as he realised that the situation had become dangerously out of control, he called for the army. But it took time for the troops to be deployed and order to be restored. In the meantime, over 3,000 innocent Sikhs were murdered and a community already reeling from the shock of Operation Blue Star was further alienated.

* * *

Rajiv Gandhi knew that he did not have long in office before an election was due. He also knew that the sympathy for the Congress and his family would evaporate in a matter of months. But he had other concerns. It is hard now to imagine how the world saw India in those dangerous days in November 1984 as Delhi burnt. Already, many global commentators had concluded that Khalistan was inevitable. Could this be followed by a larger break up of India? Would the Centre hold?

What we underestimate in most assessments of the 1984 election is the extent to which Rajiv set out to provide hope. Despite the tragedy of his mother's assassination and the massacres that followed, he seemed energetic and resolute. Moreover, he was both young and charismatic. Rather than promise more of the same, he offered an alternative to Mrs Gandhi's style of politics. He talked of the computer revolution, of preparing India for the twenty-first century and for our country to assume its rightful place among the great nations of the world.

This message was combined with the most clever and sophisticated electoral campaign ever devised for an Indian election. Advertising agencies had always had some role to play in Indian politics but this time around, the Congress brought in a prominent company from Mumbai called Rediffusion and gave it a free hand in sculpting the message.The agency's market research demonstrated that the greater fear in the hearts of voters was a horror of instability and the danger of India breaking up. Accordingly it designed a sharp, good looking campaign which first presented the danger and then made it clear that only Rajiv's Congress could hold India together. We will never know how much the campaign swung public opinion but it was clear that for the first time an Indian election was being fought like one in the West, with a control message that emerged out of opinion polls and was reflected in speeches, slogans, hoardings and newspaper ads.

But this was not going to be enough, or so the Congress believed. It was also necessary to humble the opposition by targeting its top leaders. Therefore, Rajiv's aide, Arun Nehru drew up a list of opposition figures who were highly respected or who had seemed like a nuisance. Then a strategy was devised to defeat each one of them.

Atal Bihari Vajpayee stood from Gwalior because he was sure that the Congress did not have a strong candidate to field against him in his home town. But at the last minute, just before nominations closed and when it was too late for Vajpayee to find another constituency, the erstwhile king, Madhavrao Scindia declared that he would contest from Gwalior. In Allahabad, H N Bahuguna seemed in a comfortable position till the Congress declared that the movie superstar, Amitabh Bachchan was joining politics and would fight Bahuguna. In Mumbai, another actor and a Gandhi family loyalist, Sunil Dutt was drafted to fight Ram Jethmalani who had been a thorn in the Gandhi family's side since the Emergency.

When the results were declared, they confounded everyone's expectations. Rajiv Gandhi and the Congress had won the single largest mandate in Indian electoral history with a staggering 50.7 per cent of the vote and 416 seats in the Lok Sabha. Not only had every opposition leader of consequence been defeated, but the opposition itself barely made it to parliament. The BJP won just two seats and Charan Singh's party, Lok Dal won a mere three.

It was partly the sympathy factor, and partly the fear that India was breaking up. But mostly, the victory was Rajiv Gandhi's own triumph. It showed how he had connected with the electorate and promised a break with the old ways. His promise was both seductive and sensible: change but with continuity.

He was now the most popular prime minister India had ever seen. Over the next five years, he could transform India. Or the pulls and pressures of Indian politics would transform Rajiv Gandhi.

As it turned out, Rajiv's popularity was transformed much more than the country he ruled.

Chapter Four

Camelot

Can any Prime Minister have won an election with as much goodwill as Rajiv Gandhi did? Jawaharlal Nehru perhaps. But the victory that Rajiv won in 1984, even topped anything that his grandfather had achieved. The Congress won 416 seats with a whopping 50.7 per cent of the vote. It was the greatest mandate ever handed to a political party by the people of India.

Only six month before, as the Congress was being soundly defeated in by-elections and assembly polls, the mood had seemed different. Then, it seemed completely unlikely that Indira Gandhi could have won a victory of any kind. But so great was India's need to believe, to re-assure itself that it was not the collapsing basket case that the international press wrote about, that the electorate decided to put its faith in the largely untested Rajiv, who, only a few years before, had been a reluctant politician.

To his credit, Rajiv Gandhi recognised the weight of expectations and moved quickly to deliver. He took on the political problems that his mother had made a mess of and tried hard to resolve them. The Akalis were brought back to the political mainstream and Rajiv signed an accord with Sant Harchand Singh Longowal, then the most important Sikh leader in India. After the accord, he announced fresh elections and an end to Central rule in Punjab.

In Assam, he followed a similar strategy of talking to the agitating students and bringing them within the political fold. The students party, Assam Gana Parishad or AGP announced it would contest assembly elections, which in due course, it won and Prafulla Mahanta, one of the agitating students became Chief Minister of Assam.

He even reached further back into the history of India's disputes and resolved the Mizo problem which had been festering since the late Sixties. He held talks with Laldenga, leader of the outlawed Mizo National Front (MNF) and persuaded him to join mainstream politics. In return, Laldenga became Chief Minister of Mizoram and after decades of violence, the insurgency finally ended. He granted statehood to Arunachal Pradesh, a sensitively located state on the border with China and made the people feel they were a part of India. You could argue (though strangely enough, the Congress does not make this claim) that one reason why we see so many young people from the North East in Delhi, Bengaluru, Mumbai and other Indian metropolitan cities is because

Rajiv Gandhi made the north eastern states feel like part of the Indian mainstream.

And then there was the economic agenda. Hard as this is to believe now, Rajiv Gandhi was the first prime minister of India who had actually done something else with his life before joining politics. He was the first Indian prime minister to have ever held down a job, put his salary cheque in the bank and paid income tax and provident fund. He was the first one to have gone to a well-known Indian school—in his case, the Doon School, a boarding school in Dehradun—and the only one to have close friends from his schooldays who had nothing to do with politics.

Some of this influenced Rajiv's economic thinking. He appointed V P Singh, a politician from UP who was known for his financial integrity, as his Finance Minister and asked him to open up the economy. Income tax rates were slashed, foreign investors were made to feel more welcome and the process of dismantling the Socialist controls that Indira Gandhi and her advisors had strangled the economy with, finally began.

But none of this was enough for the new prime minister. In his speeches he acted as though the twentieth century was no more than a springboard to the future. The important thing he said, was that India became a global superpower in the twenty-first century. The country, he said, missed the industrial revolution because of colonisation, but we could not afford to miss the electronic revolution. By the twenty-first century, India should be an IT superpower, a nation where young people were computer literate, where Indian IT professionals were regarded as being among the best in the world.

In retrospect, this seems like a remarkably far-sighted policy. But at the time, Rajiv was roundly lampooned for depending too much on technology and opposition leaders joked that the real leader of India was not Rajivji but Computerji.

Looking back on the first two years of Rajiv Gandhi's reign, it does really seem as though the slogan the press frequently used in that era, Camelot, was somehow appropriate. For educated Indians things had never been better. Finally, there was a prime minister who seemed articulate, sophisticated, globally-aware and above all, decent.

But then, things began to go wrong. Eventually Rajiv Gandhi failed as a Prime Minister not because he looked too far ahead into the twenty-first century but because he had not grasped how to handle those very twentieth century issues: corruption and communalism.

Of the two, the corruption issue was the murkiest. Asked to open up the economy, Finance Minister V P Singh decided to take on the corporate sector. His tax sleuths launched a new raid raj where India's top industrialists were arrested and had their premises searched. Vijay Mallya was unnecessarily humiliated; a senior figure like L M Thapar was jailed; even S L Kirloskar, the grand old man of Indian industry was grilled by tax inspectors though his group had one of the cleanest images in India.

V P Singh also inserted himself into a long-running corporate battle between Nusli Wadia, the aristocratic owner of Bombay Dyeing, once India's top textile company and Dhirubhai Ambani of Reliance. Ambani was India's fastest growing industrialist with a reputation for being able to manipulate the license permit raj to his advantage.

Wadia hated Ambani and thought he was a crook. V P Singh agreed and joined forces with Wadia in trying to pull Ambani down. V P Singh's officers went after Ambani with such vigour that the middle-aged businessman suffered a stroke and was taken to hospital in San Diego. The running of his empire fell to his sons, Mukesh and Anil, both then in their Twenties.

As V P Singh's raid raj and the Ambani-Wadia battle hit the headline, there was a new development. Rajiv's single closest friend was the actor Amitabh Bachchan. At Rajiv's urging, Bachchan had stood for election from Allahabad, defeating H N Bahuguna and people even talked about Bachchan as a potential prime minister. If anything were to happen to Rajiv, people said, Amitabh will have to take over.

Bachchan laughed off all such talk but it struck a chord with V P Singh whose political base was, after all, Allahabad. By the end of 1985, a whispering campaign against Bachchan, encouraged by V P Singh's aides, had begun. Was he the money man of the Rajiv regime? Why had his brother, Ajitabh become a Non Resident and chosen to live in Switzerland. And so on.

Given this background, it was easy enough for people to tell Rajiv that V P Singh was actually plotting a coup in tandem with Arun Nehru, Rajiv's cousin and a political heavyweight. V P Singh's acolytes, the Prime Minister was told, were looking for evidence against Bachchan that would embarrass Rajiv. And they had hired private detectives abroad to look into Sonia Gandhi's family.

Was any of this true? When I interviewed him during that period, V P Singh swore to me that he had never dreamt of investigating Sonia and Rajiv and claimed that stories to this effect were part of the misinformation being spread by the Ambanis. He was more circumspect when it came to Amitabh however and one could tell that he was keen to dig the knife into the superstar at the first opportunity he got.

We'll never know whether Rajiv Gandhi fell prey to misinformation or whether there were things he knew but chose not to share. First, he sidelined Arun Nehru. Then, he moved V P Singh out of Finance and into Defence. Though Rajiv later told me that V P Singh and he had a heart-to-heart chat the day before the latter was moved to Defence and that there was no ill-will, that was not how V P Singh saw it.

One of the first things he did, on getting to the Defence Ministry, in 1987, was to announce an inquiry into kickbacks in the HDW Submarine deal. According to Singh, arms dealers had made millions by acting as middlemen. Normally, this would not have been a big deal but the Rajiv Gandhi government had taken the unusual step of banning all agents in defence deals. This was more symbolic than practical. All over the world, the arms business operates through agents. And all that the government achieved by banning agents was that the dealers worked far from public view, ensuring that there was no transparency at all.

But if agents had benefitted from the HDW deal, this was against the stated policy of the government. Congressmen understood at once what V P Singh was trying to do. Having been moved out of Finance, he was now trying to find evidence of corruption in defence deals. That way, he could cement his credentials as the cabinet's Mr Clean and suggest—by implication—that the reason Rajiv did not like him was because he was getting too close to Rajiv's own secrets.

It was one of those decisive moments in history. Now that V P Singh had more or less come out openly against the government he was part of, there could be only one of the two outcomes. Either Singh would bring Rajiv down. Or Rajiv would finish off V P Singh. At the time, the advantage was with Rajiv. He had over 400 MPs in the Lok Sabha. He was the most popular prime minister in history. He did not need to be worried about unsubstantiated allegations made by a disgruntled colleague.

But then, out of nowhere, came a bolt of lightening that changed everything. In the spring of 1987, Swedish Radio reported that the Swedish arms company, Bofors had paid bribes to secure a contract to supply guns to the Indian army in 1986. Swedish Radio was investigating Bofors—as was the Swedish government—so the India allegation was just one of many charges. Judging by the Swedish inquiry, Bofors had paid bribes to many other countries and the Indian kickbacks were not particularly sensational.

But given the mood in India and the fuss over the HDW inquiry, the new charges came as a godsend to V P Singh. Here, at least, was independent verification of the claims he was making.

Nobody has ever been able to explain to me why Rajiv Gandhi handled the Bofors matter so badly. All he needed to have said was that, as far as he knew, no bribes had been paid but now that Swedish Radio had made this charge, he would order a full inquiry. That was all he needed to do.

Instead, he went public saying that no commissions had been paid on the deal, thereby rebutting a charge that had not even been made. Swedish Radio was concerned with bribes not legitimate business commissions. Besides, how did Rajiv know whether commissions had been paid or not? That was between Bofors and its agents, whoever they were.

But because Rajiv had moved the goal-posts, his opponents now had the easier task of merely proving that commissions had in fact been paid. That was all they needed to do to prove that Rajiv was wrong. It was no longer necessary to even look for evidence of bribery or corruption, let alone find a trail that led to Rajiv or to his government.

V P Singh and the opposition fell on the Swedish Radio charges like hungry men at a feast. As Rajiv's government continued to make one blunder after another, the scandal grew. And at each stage, the government overreacted even claiming that the Swedish Radio charges were part of a Western campaign to discredit India.

In the public mind, V P Singh, Rajiv, HDW, Bofors and the Bachchans all became jumbled up. V P Singh resigned from the government and declared that he had been forced out because the corrupt Congress regime was taking bribes and entrusting the money to Amitabh Bachchan for safe-keeping. All this without a shred of evidence.

But perhaps there was something to hide even if it did not directly implicate Rajiv Gandhi. G Parthasarathy was Rajiv Gandhi's Media Advisor during the second part of Rajiv's term and used to deal with Mohan Katre, the then Director of CBI who was investigating Bofors.

Parthasarathy says that Katre told him, after he returned from Switzerland where he met Swiss authorities, that he had been assured that none of the payments from Bofors had any connection to Rajiv Gandhi. The Swiss could not understand what the fuss in India was about.

But there was a problem. Though the Swiss have a long and complicated legal process to complete before they can hand over any information about numbered accounts, they are often willing to share—off-the-record and in confidence—the details of bank deposits with investigating officers from other countries.

So the Swiss told Katre into whose accounts the payments had been made. One of them was Ottavio Quattrocchi.

And that was the problem.

Quattrocchi was the Indian representative of Snamprogetti, an Italian government-owned infrastructure company. He had lived in India since the 1950s and when Sonia Gandhi first moved to Delhi, the Quattrocchis had been friendly and welcoming to another Italian in a strange land. Over the years, the friendship between the Quattrocchis and the Gandhis had grown to the extent that Delhi resounded with gossip about Quattrocchi's activities. It was often suggested that even though he was a salaried employee of Snamprogetti, Quattrocchi inserted himself into many other deals. He told visiting foreign businessmen that he knew the Indian system well—which he did—and would advise them on how to get contracts out of the Indian government.

Rajiv was sensitive to the criticism of Quattrocchi and when the HBJ pipeline was being constructed in the 1980s, he gave clear instructions that the contract was not to be awarded to Snamprogetti because of the Quattrocchi connection—an instruction Quattrocchi received with much bitterness.

The Swiss told Katre that Quattrocchi had received some of the Bofors commissions. The money had not moved out of Quattrocchi's account to any other account so he was clearly not a conduit for kickbacks to somebody else. The money was his. And he had, presumably, got the commission because he had worked as an agent for Bofors.

Says Parthasarathy, 'The Gandhis had allowed Quattrocchi to be seen to be too close to them. And if it got out that Quattrocchi was one of the agents, it would have been very difficult to explain. And that really was the cause for the confusion on Bofors.'

* * *

Meanwhile another drama was playing itself out. During Indira Gandhi's time, Rajiv Gandhi, Arun Nehru and their friends had picked three people close to Mrs Gandhi as their enemies. One of them was Pranab Mukherjee. Despite being Mrs Gandhi's number two, he was sent to West Bengal to be Pradesh Congress Committee or PCC chief and when the Congress lost a municipal election in the state, Arun Nehru called him up late one night, shouted at him and told him to resign from even that minor post.

But Pranab got off lightly. R K Dhawan had been Indira Gandhi's closest aide. But not only did the new regime throw him out, it went to the unprecedented extent of framing him for Mrs Gandhi's assassination. An inquiry report written by Justice Thakkar said that Dhawan's role in the murder needed to be probed and though the charge was outrageous, Dhawan spent years in a living hell before the CBI team probing Mrs Gandhi's murder stood up for his innocence.

But the most complicated and crucial relationship was the one between President Zail Singh and the Prime Minister. Rajiv had never liked Zail Singh but he now began to develop utter contempt for him. He believed that Zail Singh had played a dubious role in Punjab affairs and began refusing him the access to government papers that is normally the President's prerogative. He knew that Zail Singh's term would end in 1987 and decided to sit it out, waiting for the next President to reach Rashtrapati Bhavan.

But Zail Singh was not without resources. He let it be known that unless he got a second term, he would create a situation that could lead to the overthrow of Rajiv's government. This was without precedent. Rajiv Gandhi was the legally elected Prime Minister of India. How could the President possibly dismiss him?

I met Zail Singh several times during this period and my guess was that he knew that the country would not have allowed him to sack Rajiv. Kuldip Nayar who knew the President well shares that assessment.

But Zail Singh's believed he could threaten to destroy Rajiv's prime ministership. From 1986 onwards, he turned Rashtrapati Bhavan into a salon where dodgy godmen like the infamous Chandraswami and various opposition leaders would conspire against the government. Throughout it all, he kept a channel open to Rajiv with a clear message. If the government would give him a second term, then Zail Singh would fall in line.

In the process, Zail Singh helped construct a coalition of those who were hostile to Rajiv, including Ramnath Goenka, proprietor of *The Indian Express* who believed, along with V P Singh, that Rajiv was not being tough enough on Dhirubhai Ambani; dissidents within the Congress; assorted anti-Congress lawyers and wheeler-dealers and much of the official opposition.

The basic charge was one of corruption and the primary target, Amitabh Bachchan. He was actually a soft target. He didn't need politics or the bad name and in any case, Rajiv's other friends, people like Arun Singh had already turned against him. So one fine day, Amitabh Bachchan wrote out a resignation letter, gave it to Rajiv, abandoned the Lok Sabha and went back to his home in Bombay's Juhu Vile Parle Scheme. His exit caused a stir and began to make Rajiv's regime seem more vulnerable.

Rajiv rode out Bachchan's departure and managed to get rid of Zail Singh but his problems were mounting. In Punjab, terrorism had received a new fillip and militants were back inside the Golden Temple. This time around, Rajiv decided that he was not going to ask the army to clear the temple. The National Security Guard or NSG would handle it. Ved Marwah was now Director-General of the NSG and he was put in charge of Operation Black Thunder, a sophisticated successor to the chaotic Operation Blue Star.

Marwah had learnt from the army's mistake during the earlier operation. He turned to the Intelligence Bureau or IB for help and in one of its greatest triumphs, it infiltrated a middle-level officer called Ajit Doval (now the National Security Advisor) into the Golden Temple. Doval was clearly not a Sikh so he had to find another excuse for being there. 'I told them I was Pakistani,' Doval says. 'I said that I had been sent by Pakistan to help them.'

So good was Doval's cover that the militants believed him and admitted him to their inner circle. Doval managed to get hold of their strategy, assessed their areas of strength and weakness and passed the information onto Marwah's NSG.

Now, armed with accurate intelligence, Marwah attacked the areas where the militants were holed up. As he says, 'This created so much panic among them that they did what we had feared. They went and took shelter in the Harmandir Sahib.'

The militants knew that after the fiasco that had led the army to destroy the Akal Takht, the NSG would not dare attack and damage the Harmandir Sahib. Marwah went to Rajiv Gandhi. He asked for direct authority, cutting out the Punjab police and the civil administration. 'I told him that I will take personal responsibility that the Harmandir Sahib will not be damaged in any way.'

To everyone's surprise, not only did Rajiv give Marwah that authority, he also involved himself in the nitty-gritty of the operation, working with the NSG on a plan to flush out the militants. Marwah sat patiently for a while till eventually the militants came out of the temple with their hands up and surrendered.

There was no damage to the Golden Temple and no unnecessary civilian casualties. Black Thunder was as much of a triumph as Blue Star had been a fiasco.

There was a problem in Sri Lanka too. Indira Gandhi's government had helped train Tamil rebels and had intervened in the civil war between the Sinhala majority and Tamil minority. Rajiv Gandhi believed, reasonably enough, that India should not be encouraging militancy in a neighbouring country and called all the Tamil groups together to seek a peaceful solution. A compromise was worked out whereby the Tamil militants would lay down their arms in return for more autonomy for the Tamil areas of Sri Lanka. The Indian army would set up a peace keeping force to supervise the ceasefire.

But the agreement pleased nobody. The Sri Lankans saw India as the enemy and as a result, Rajiv was attacked by a naval rating when he was inspecting a guard of honour in Sri Lanka. The Tamils, initially pretending to go along with the ceasefire, held on to their weapons and then took to attacking the Indian Peace Keeping Force or IPKF. All in all, it was a complete mess. The Indian army ended up losing soldiers to a bunch of militants who had originally been trained and armed by India!

As worrying as these developments were, they paled in comparison to the big issue that would dominate Rajiv's last years in office. The Congress had always—and especially since the time Mrs Gandhi first split the party—seen itself as the champion of the minorities.

This was a safe position to take because none of the opposition parties were hostile to the minorities. In terms of the secularism issue, Janata Party had followed more or less the same policies as the Congress. Even the Jan Sangh component of the old Janata Party had not taken a particularly pro-Hindu position and when the Bharatiya Janata Party or BJP was created in 1980, its leader A B Vajpayee made it clear that he believed in a Nehruvian view of secularism.

The one blip in the communal situation had been the Khalistan movement. But even there, the dispute had not influenced mainstream politics. The Akalis had never taken an anti-Hindu position and the other parties refused to exploit any Hindu-Sikh divide for political gain.

But things were changing as Rajiv was soon to discover. The Shah Bano case seems almost insignificant if you consider the specifics. An elderly man called Mohammed Ahmed Khan appealed to the Supreme Court against a lower court's order that he would have to pay maintenance to his divorced wife, a lady called Shah Bano. Khan claimed that under the Muslim Personal law, he only had to pay her maintenance for three months, which he had done. The Supreme Court ruled against Khan arguing that Section 125 of the Criminal Procedure Code, which gave Shah Bano the right to regular maintenance, overruled Muslim Personal Law whenever there was a conflict between the two.

The amount involved was a trifle. After the judgement, Shah Bano received a maintenance of only ₹ 179.20 paise per month. Neither were Mohammed Khan and Shah Bano public figures. But Muslim leaders took umbrage at the suggestion that anything could have precedence over their Personal Law. All over India, mullahs and maulvis raised the cry that Islam was under threat.

In response to this uproar, a Muslim MP called G M Banatwalla moved a private members bill in parliament seeking to exempt Muslims from the provisions of Section 125 of the Criminal Procedure Code. The government decided, quite reasonably to oppose the bill and to support the Supreme Court judgement. The then Minister of State for Home Affairs, Arif Mohammad Khan told parliament that the Quran required Muslims to respect divorced women and with the government voting against it, the bill was defeated.

This had the effect of enraging Muslim clerics and even mainstream Muslim leaders who claimed that an interference in Personal Law marked an assault on the rights of the Muslim community. Confronted with this uproar, Rajiv executed an about-turn. A few months later, the Congress introduced a bill of its own seeking to do exactly what Banatwalla had wanted: taking Muslims out of the preview of Section 125. A humiliated Arif Mohammad Khan had no choice but to resign.

Why had Rajiv backtracked? Why did he go against his own instincts? Why had he succumbed to the pressure of the mullahs? The uncharitable view is that his advisors told him he was losing Muslim support, crucial at the polls. The charitable explanation is that with over 400 seats in parliament, he did not really have to care about a few noisy mullahs but come to the sincere conclusion that the Muslim community needed to be re-assured that in Hindu majority India its rights and, in particular, its Personal Law, would be protected. Either way, it was a terrible mistake.

Shahid Siddiqui, editor of *Nai Duniya*, knew Rajiv well and was consulted by him on the case. Siddiqui says that he advised Rajiv Gandhi not to touch the Muslim Personal Law. 'Even educated persons like me and Salman Khurshid felt threatened. Somewhere in our psyche was the idea that in Hindu-majority India, it will be the majority that will be ruling and Muslims will not be able to practice Islam. We felt that even if this was a minor matter, once a small window was opened then the whole idea of Shariyat or whatever is left of it in this country will be endangered.'

It was this kind of advice that led Rajiv to change his mind on the Shah Bano case.

Just as Muslim clerics were agitated over an issue that seemed minor at first, Hindu saints and sadhus now found an issue of their own. The dispute over a mosque in Ayodhya dated back to the nineteenth century. Some Hindus claimed that this was the birthplace of Lord Ram, or Ram Janmabhoomi. The mosque that stood on that site, they said, was built by the Emperor Babar after destroying a Hindu temple that had originally been located on the spot.

The problem with the dispute was that historical verification was hard to find. Even if a historical Lord Ram did exist, there were other places that also claimed to be his birthplace. And if a Hindu temple had actually been destroyed in the Mughal period, well, that was history. Buddhist temples were destroyed by Hindus and Hindu temples by Muslims. Nobody could really go back in history and rebuild every single destroyed temple.

In 1949, an idol of the infant Ram was smuggled into the mosque. Sadhus claimed it had materialised miraculously and new communal clashes broke out. Finally, the administration issued an order allowing the worship of the idol on a single day each year. This arrangement persisted till February 1986 when a district judge ordered that Hindus should be permitted to worship the idol on a regular basis. The judge was acting in response to an appeal from the Vishwa Hindu Parishad or VHP, an RSS-affiliate which had mobilised sadhus to reclaim the Ram Janmabhoomi site. But was the judge acting on his own? It was whispered that he had been directed to issue his order by ministers close to Rajiv Gandhi, including Arun Nehru. Apparently, the government felt that having pleased Muslim mullahs, it now needed to offer a sop to Hindu sadhus.

But the sadhus were not content with a mere sop. The VHP now began an agitation demanding that the mosque either be demolished or moved so that a grand Ram Temple could be constructed on the spot. For the vast majority of Hindus, all this came as a surprise. Till the agitation broke out again in the 1980s, hardly anyone had even heard of the Babri Masjid or of any sacred birthplace of Ram. This was not some holy spot venerated by hundreds of millions of India's Hindus. Rather it was a place they were only just hearing about.

And yet, the Ram Janmabhoomi agitation touched a chord throughout North India. What gave the issue its power? There were many reasons but two seem significant. The first was a question of timing. India was rediscovering Lord Ram. A TV serial based on the Ramayan, telecast on India's only TV network, the state-owned Doordarshan, had become a rage. Hindus were intrigued to discover that there was an actual spot where Ram was said to have been born. And they were angered when they heard that a temple built on the site had been destroyed by Muslim invaders and that a mosque now stood on the spot. The VHP worked hard at re-opening the wounds of old, with stories of how Hindus had been mistreated by Muslim rulers.

A second reason was that there seemed to be a conflict between the rhetoric of twenty-first century India and the grim reality of Indian politics. How could a government that was committed to modernisation deny a Muslim woman the right to a pitifully small sum as maintenance only because a few medieval-minded mullahs created a fuss? The reality, or so the VHP claimed was that the Congress stayed in office only by playing vote-bank politics. The mullahs were important because they could deliver the votes of millions of uneducated Muslims. Hindus, on the other hand, constituted no single vote-bank controlled by any kind of clergy. And so Hindus lost out to Muslims in electoral calculations.

The amazing thing about the growing politicisation of Hindus is that nobody in the Congress noticed at first how strong the level of anger was. And the Muslim leadership did not help. Almost as though they were working to a script written by the RSS, the mullahs began claiming that the dispute over the Babri Masjid was yet another assault on India's Muslims. Some mullahs demanded that the government now allow the reading of namaaz in historic mosques controlled by the Archaeological Survey of India or ASI. If these demands were not met, they threatened, Indian Muslims would boycott Republic Day.

This was the time for the government to have held firm. But it bended over backwards—just as it had done in the Shah Bano case—to be fair to the minorities. When the expatriate Indian author, Salman Rushdie published a novel called *The Satanic Verses*, Syed Shahabuddin, a Muslim politician who had not even read the book, called for it to be banned on the grounds that it would offend Muslims. The government promptly banned its import. Even then, Muslim leaders whipped up a frenzy among their supporters and led angry demonstrations against Rushdie. One Muslim academic who said that he was uncomfortable with the banning of books was promptly beaten up by his students. Liberal Muslim leaders refused to support him.

Within the BJP, things were changing. The liberal Atal Bihari Vajpayee had been sidelined. His protégé, L K Advani was now the party's leader and he sensed an opportunity in the growing Hindu backlash. As the VHP's Ayodhya movement grew in strength, Advani associated the BJP with it and then, effectively hijacked the issue. He set out on a rath yatra, complete with an actor dressed as Ram and set out to inflame Hindu sentiments.

* * *

By 1988, Rajiv Gandhi was a Prime Minister under siege. The Bofors issue simply would not go away. The Swedish armament giant conceded that it had paid commissions to middlemen—contrary to what Rajiv had claimed—

but insisted that there were just "winding-up charges" prior to sacking these middlemen in accordance with the Indian government's demands. Though there was still no evidence linking Rajiv or anyone in the Congress to the deal, there was a feeling that the government was trying to cover-up the truth so that the middlemen could get away.

Then, there was the problem with the prime minister's inner circle. The people who had been Rajiv's friends and advisors had now really all gone. Arun Nehru had left the Congress and joined up with V P Singh and Arif Mohammad Khan. Amitabh Bachchan was back in Bombay trying to pick up the pieces of his movie career. Arun Singh, Rajiv's childhood buddy who had been his closest advisor in government was gone too, choosing to resign when Rajiv was particularly vulnerable, giving the impression, perhaps unintentionally, that he was disillusioned with what his old friend was doing.

Desperate, Rajiv turned back to the people his mother had relied on. In an incredible twist, R K Dhawan was brought back and ensconced in his old role at Prime Minister's house. Even Pranab Mukherjee was sent for and asked for advice on economic matters. As V P Singh travelled the country claiming that Rajiv and his friends (Amitabh Bachchan was a favourite target) were corrupt, L K Advani rode the Hindu backlash, taking the BJP to a poll position from the mess into which it had sunk after the 1984 election debacle.

The government was now reduced to trying to reach some kind of an arrangement with the VHP over the Ram Janmabhoomi issue. G Parthasarathy, a member of Rajiv's PMO, says that Buta Singh, the then Home

Minister was asked to tell the BJP that the government would permit the sangh parivar to conduct a shilanyas or a foundation stone laying ceremony at the site. But says Parthasarathy, there were two conditions. The first was that the ceremony would not take place on disputed land. The second was that while they would be allowed to lay the foundation stone, no actual construction would be allowed.

But everything went wrong. First, says Parthasarathy, 'The VHP went on to start construction. This went against a High Court order and had to be stopped. Secondly, the ceremony was supposed to be on undisputed land but they got the locations wrong. It was on WAQF land. So the government got taken for a ride and ended up earning the wrath of both communities.'

As the election neared, Rajiv began to seem like a lonely and desolate figure, a victim at the mercy of forces he could no longer control. He had taken office determined to change the system. And in some ways, he had. To his credit he had cleaned up the messes his mother left behind in Assam and Punjab. He had pushed the economy towards liberalisation and he had focussed on the software and technological revolution that he was sure would dominate the next two decades.

But he had failed at all the things that politicians are supposed to understand. He had no clue how to handle minority concerns and listened first to one advisor and then to another, giving the impression that he did not know what he was doing. Stuck in the Prime Minister's house, he had no idea of the growing wave of Hindu anger and impatience. And having depended on friends who were as out of their depth as him, he completely failed to counter the perception that his government had profited from arms deals as Bofors.

When the 1989 election was called, everyone agreed that the Congress would be battered. But would it lose its majority? After all, when you start out with 400 plus seats, you can afford to lose a hundred or so and still hold on to your majority.

But when the tide has turned, when events have slipped out of control and when there's no one you can really depend on, then disaster is inevitable. When the results were declared it turned out that the Congress had lost more than a hundred seats. In fact it had lost more than 200. It had gone from having more than 400 MPs to having to content itself with 197.

It was a small consolation but nobody else had won the election either. V P Singh and his allies in the old Janata grouping (their party was called the Janata Dal) had won less seats than the Congress: they had 143. The BJP had come out of nowhere to win 86. And the Communists had around 50.

In other words, parliament was dangerously hung. No stable government seemed possible. And India had entered a new and dangerous era of uncertainty.

Chapter Five

Mandal & Mandir

In 1977, the Janata Party had been offered a historic opportunity to give India its first non-Congress government and had messed it up. It had taken Indira Gandhi and the Congress less than three years to climb back into office. Now, as the results of the 1989 election came streaming in, it was clear that more than a decade later, the people of India were offering non-Congress forces another chance.

But this time, the verdict was not as decisive as it had been in 1977. For a start, the Congress was still the largest party in the Lok Sabha with 197 seats. No other party had anything like a majority. And worse still, even if two large parties aligned, they still could not form a government.

Faced with this nearly impossible situation, the opposition struck a strange but necessary compromise. The Janata Dal would form the next government. The BJP would support it from the outside and so would the Left. Could the Left and BJP really agree on anything? Probably not. But at least for now they agreed that the election results had been a call for a non-Congress government.

The new government began its tenure with a lie and a confidence trick. Chandrashekhar, who had been President of the Janata Party since 1977 expected to be prime minister. But V P Singh had become the face of opposition to Rajiv Gandhi. So perhaps the sub-text of the verdict had been a call for him to become prime minister. One way of settling the issue would have been to hold a free election. But just as the Janata Party had refused to allow a leadership election in 1977, so was the mood of the party against internal democracy. Instead it was decided that the party would play a trick on Chandrashekhar. He would be told that Devi Lal, the farmers' leader from Haryana would be the new prime minister and would even be asked to propose Devi Lal's candidacy. But Devi Lal had been briefed. The moment he got the job, he was to get up and say that he wanted V P Singh to be prime minister. V P Singh would accept the responsibility and Chandrashekhar would be left looking like an idiot.

Kuldip Nayar who was very close to Janata Dal leaders, remembers the day. 'I told Devi Lal that there was an incident in the Mahabharat when an elephant died. And the elephant had the same name—Ashwathama —as a warrior. And they managed to create confusion around that name,' remembers Nayar. 'So I told Devi Lal, it does matter whether you became prime minister for one minute or ten years. Sometimes it is good to tell a half-truth. You have been made prime minister, but you chose to give the post to V P Singh.'

Years later, I asked Chandrashekhar about the incident. He said categorically, 'V P Singh's election as Prime Minister was, by any standards, illegal. Because if one person is elected, then it's not a crown that he can hand over to somebody else.'

So why didn't Chandrashekhar challenge the election? 'There was so much pressure on me to formally oppose the election,' he said. 'But I did not want to make an issue of it. Because I knew that at that time people had voted for a non-Congress government.'

There may have been another reason for Chandrashekhar's silence. His close associate, Kamal Morarka remembers the day: 'Two hours after the election, I met him at his home. He said, "Kamal, it is just as well. If there had been an incident, this is what the result would have been. I would not have won. But now they have betrayed me so the ball is in their court." He was philosophical.'

V P Singh had been elected on an anti-corruption agenda and was determined to pursue it while in office. So, rather tend to the growing crisis in the Indian economy, his first priority was to prosecute Rajiv Gandhi. Investigators were sent to Switzerland to try and trace the Bofors payment and foreign governments were asked to investigate Sonia Gandhi's sisters and their husbands. Another track of inquiry was the Bachchans. V P Singh's sleuths put it out that one of the Bofors accounts had been traced to Ajitabh Bachchan and Amitabh became the government's primary target.

All this yielded limited results. Try as they might, the investigators could not find a scrap of paper linking Rajiv Gandhi to any kickback. Ajitabh Bachchan was so angered by suggestions that he had received payments from Bofors that he filed a defamation suit against a Swedish newspaper that had reported the existence of a secret Swiss bank account in his name. On the very first day of the trial, the Swedish newspaper conceded it had been misled by Indian investigators, apologised to the Bachchans and agreed to pay damages. The outcome of the case had one unforeseen consequence. Amitabh, who had seen all his films flop for three years, suddenly found that his box-office fortunes had changed. A really terrible movie called *Aaj Ka Arjun*, that was his next release went on to become a super hit and a few months later, *Hum* became one of the biggest ever hits.

With his anti-corruption agenda backfiring, V P Singh looked desperately for another issue to cling on to. On 15 August 1990, during his Independence Day speech, he told India that he had found it.

V P Singh's new crusade was on behalf of the backward castes. The Prime Minister dredged up a largely forgotten report filed by the Mandal Commission. This suggested that the principle of reservation in government jobs, restricted so far to Scheduled Castes and Tribes should now be extended to include the so-called backward castes.

There were three problems with the proposal. The first was that V P Singh himself had never before embraced this issue. He had rarely spoken about it nor had it played any part in the Janata Dal's election campaign so he could hardly claim that he had a mandate to implement the Mandal recommendations. The second problem was that many people were already worried about the existing system of reservations. The constitution of India had intended reservations to be time-bound. Yet no politician had the guts to say when they would end. Now, rather than phasing reservations out, V P Singh was actually extending them to include new castes.

And the third problem was that not everyone believed that the backward castes, as defined by Mandal, were really that backward. Many of them were well off and powerful and some of them were actually the castes that were most associated with atrocities against Dalits.

But the contrary argument was simple and urgent. It could be summed up in one word: expediency. If the backward castes decided to vote for V P Singh out of gratitude, then the Prime Minister had built himself a strong new constituency overnight. He no longer had to worry about middle class approval or to pursue the failing anti-corruption agenda.

The middle class was not pleased by this change of direction. It felt angry and betrayed by a man it had once hailed as an anti-corruption messiah. Overnight, the mood of the media changed. Commentators who had praised V P Singh as a modern-day Gandhi turned viciously against him. But the strongest reaction came from students at India's leading universities.

To V P Singh's surprise, the decision to implement Mandal Commission's recommendations, caused an explosion of rage among India's youth. Colleges were shut as students took to the streets to protest. Then, as the nation watched in horror, the protests took an unexpected turn: students started burning themselves alive.

Why did Mandal provoke such anger among India's students? You could argue that it was because further reservation adversely affected their employment prospects though, once the immolations began, a frantic government clarified that the Mandal proposals only affected 40,000 public sector jobs.

My view has always been that the protests represented something more visceral and basic. By 1990, the hope of the Eighties had been snuffed out. There was a real sense that the Indian dream had died and that young people really had nowhere to go. Mandal was the last straw. It convinced a new generation of frustrated Indians that politicians had no desire to build a new India for the future. They would much rather play politics and cultivate vote-banks. The protests and the immolations stemmed from that frustration, desperation even, from a belief that there was no hope, that a whole generation had been sold down the river, that in an India that was headed for the abyss, they were to be Generation Zero.

Even as Indians watched appalled when children burnt themselves alive on the streets of our cities, the BJP knew that it had a problem. If the backward caste ploy worked, then the Janata Dal had just bought itself a new vote bank. All the impressive gains that the BJP had made in recent years would now be lost in the pro-Janata Dal groundswell.

A worried L K Advani decided that it was time to revive the Ram Mandir issue. He declared that he was disappointed by the failure of V P Singh's government to adequately redress Hindu grievances and announced that he would now go on a new rath yatra.

V P Singh was not unduly concerned by this move. As Advani began talking about the need for Hindus to reclaim the Ram Janmabhoomi site, Muslims grew increasingly insecure. And that suited V P Singh fine. Having painted himself as the Messiah of the Backwards, he now declared that he was there to help the Muslims and began contacting mullahs and maulvis to win their support. V P Singh had it all figured out: even if the BJP withdrew support, the Janata Dal would do extremely well in any election because of the support of the Muslims and the backwards. It was sad that the middle class had turned against him and tragic that students were immolating themselves on the streets but hey! this was politics, right!

In October, as Advani's rath yatra moved through North India, communal tensions were inflamed. It was expected that there would be more violence and rioting before the yatra was over. But on 30 October 1990, Advani was arrested in Samastipur in Bihar on the orders of Laloo Prasad Yadav. Laloo was a Janata Dal Chief Minister and V P Singh claimed that he had ordered Laloo to arrest Advani.

Predictably, the BJP withdrew support. But this did not phase V P Singh in the slightest. He scheduled a vote of confidence which he knew he would lose. He told Muslims, '*Sarkar giregi lekin masjid nahin giregi*' (The government may fall but not the mosque). V P Singh expected that once he lost the confidence vote on 10 November, fresh elections would be called and with Muslim and backward caste support in the new Lok Sabha, the Janata Dal would win more seats than the Congress.

Perhaps this would indeed have happened. But we will never know. Because, in a moment of karmic retribution, two of the people who V P Singh had betrayed united to foil his master plan. They were, of course, Rajiv Gandhi and Chandrashekhar. The deal was as follows: Chandrashekhar would break the Janata Dal and form his own group. The Congress would support the Chandrashekhar faction of the Janata Dal from outside and Chandrashekhar would take office as the new prime minister.

And, much to V P Singh's chagrin, this is exactly what happened. Eleven months after he had taken office by playing a trick on Chandrashekhar, V P Singh was out of office. And Chandrashekhar was prime minister. Because Chandrashekhar had only 64 MPs to the Congress' 232 this was not an arrangement that could last and Chandrashekhar knew it. But he told his supporters that with children dying on the streets over Mandal and riots breaking out all over India because of the rath yatra, the time was not right for an election. So, he had agreed to hold office till tempers cooled.

Chandrashekhar told me how the deal with Rajiv Gandhi was struck: 'One late night, I got an invitation from Romesh Bhandari who was then Lt. Governor of Delhi for a cup of coffee. I am not accustomed to taking coffee late at night, so I laughed. But when I went there, Rajiv Gandhi was present. And we discussed general things. Nothing about government formation.'

Clearly, the two men were sizing each other up. Then R K Dhawan arranged a second meeting. And Chandrashekhar claimed, 'I told Rajiv I have no moral right to form a government. If elections are held at this moment then there will be a lot of bloodshed. So I don't know! I have no experiences of running a government. But I can do something to ease the situation. And it is better if you send Congressmen to join the government. If not, then tell me if you have a problem with me. Because if you do have a problem then I will try to solve it. But if you make me feel inadequate then I shall not wait for even one hour. I will resign.'

With V P Singh out of Race Course Road, the anti-Mandal protests stopped. Even the Ayodhya movement took a break. But by then, India had its own problems. Put simply, the country was broke. The Prime Minister was told by his economic advisors that India was about to default on its debt repayments. India will never default, announced Chandrashekhar and pledged part of the country's gold reserves to cover the debt.

Then, another problem broke out. The US had attacked Iraq over the invasion of Kuwait and the first Gulf War was underway. President George Bush asked Chandrashekhar if India would allow US planes to refuel here and the Prime Minister said yes. This led to howls of protest from the Congress and to the first sign that Chandrashekhar and Rajiv Gandhi were not getting along. Kamal Morarka says, there was more to it. According to Morarka, the real reason for the withdrawal of support was that Chandrashekhar seemed to be coming closer to settling the Ayodhya issue. He had summoned both sides and given them a talking-to.

'He told the RSS people that if they dared touch the structure, he would ask the police to open fire on them. Then he called the Babri Masjid Action Committee and told them "Your structure is safe. I can promise you that. But there are five lakh villages in India where Hindus and Muslims remain side-by-side. Suppose there are communal clashes throughout the country? I don't have that much police and army to protect the life of every Muslim." And in just three days, both sides began to climb down.'

Adds Morarka: 'The ground rules were that nobody would leak these discussions to the press. He used Bhairon Singh Shekhawat, the Chief Minister of Rajasthan and Sharad Pawar, Chief Minister of Maharashtra as the go-betweens. They met over 15 days at Jodhpur House. And after 15 days, they came up with a formula. The government would allot land and the masjid would be shifted there. After that a law would be passed saying that no such issue—whether in Banaras or Mathura or anywhere—would be re-opened. Simple. We had a solution.'

But, claims Morarka, that that set off another crisis. 'Sharad Pawar went and told Rajiv Gandhi. Rajiv called up Chandrashekhar and said, "Can you please wait for two days?" And in those two days he withdrew support to our government.'

Is this what really happened? Again, we will never know. But Rajiv Gandhi did withdraw support to Chandrashekhar's government and asked for fresh elections. Congressmen begged him to reconsider. Most of Chandrashekhar's MPs would back a Congress government, they said. Why didn't the Congress simply take office during this Lok Sabha? It had the numbers. No, said Rajiv, I want a mandate from the people. And so in 1991, less than two years after the last general election, India went to the polls again.

The Rajiv Gandhi who toured India tirelessly during that campaign bore little resemblance to the haughty and embattled Prime Minister of 1998-99. This Rajiv was relaxed, unfussy, willing to mingle with crowds and ready to concede that he had made mistakes during his term in office. As the campaign wore on, it became clear that Rajiv was still popular and there was no doubt that the Congress would wind up as the single largest party in the next Lok Sabha. Would it win a majority? Perhaps not. But Rajiv had verbal assurances of support from the Left so even if he had to form a minority government, he knew that he was certain to be prime minister again.

Alas it was not to be. On 21 May 1991, as part of his campaign, Rajiv drove to Sriperumbudur from Chennai where he was due to address an election meeting. Before going on to the stage, he met a few local people who had been given an opportunity to greet him personally. One of them, a woman called Dhanu, who had made her way to the enclosure by misleading a local politician, bent down to touch his feet. That was probably the last thing that Rajiv Gandhi ever saw. As she bent low, Dhanu detonated an explosive belt full of RDX that killed Rajiv, Dhanu and several others in the enclosure on the spot.

Just weeks before he would have returned to his old South Block Office, Rajiv Gandhi was dead. He was only forty-six.

His widow, Sonia remembered their last meeting in an interview to me. 'I wish I had gone to Madras with him. I had met him when he came back from Amethi and he was extremely tired. His arms and hands were swollen because people just wanted to touch him and hug him and pull him. And at that point I felt very bad seeing him in that condition and I thought of going with him. And then I thought; well, it is just going to be a question of two days. And the aeroplane had very little space. But when I heard the news, I think I just blacked out.'

News of the assassination shocked India. The Congress party went into a huddle and asked Sonia Gandhi to take his place as party president. She refused point-blank. Did she have any one else in mind? The Congress Working Committee (CWC) asked. The Congress knew, as I imagine did Sonia, that the Congress president would be the next prime minister once the results were declared. Few people know what Sonia Gandhi considered doing in that period. Natwar Singh is one of them.

'I told Sonia that she should go by the advice of P N Haksar who had been so close to Indiraji,' says Natwar. 'So I brought Haksar saab to 10 Janpath. His advice was that Aruna Asif Ali and I should go to the Vice President Shankar Dayal Sharma and request him to resign as Vice President. He would become Congress President and then, after the results were declared, Prime Minister.

'To our utter surprise, Shankar Dayal Sharma refused the suggestions. He said that his age and health would not allow him to take the job. So we went back to Haksar. He said to ask P V Narasimha Rao who had been denied a Rajya Sabha ticket by Rajiv and who had retired from politics and was leaving for Hyderabad. So Sonia said "All right, let's appoint PV."'

And so, only because Shankar Dayal Sharma turned down the job, P V Narasimha Rao became Prime Minister of India.

Rao had his work cut out. The economy had to be the first priority. India was bankrupt. It needed funds, from the IMF if it was to pay the bills. But who would be the new Finance Minister. Rao reached out to I G Patel, a former Chief Economic Advisor to the government who had gone on to senior jobs at the UN and then the London School of Economics. But Patel said he did not want the post.

So Dr Manmohan Singh became Finance Minister of India. All his life, this mild-mannered bureaucrat had followed a vaguely Left-wing line. But now the IMF held a gun to his head. If India did not liberalise, then the IMF would not provide the funds required for the country's survival.

Nobody had expected two old men—Narasimha Rao and Manmohan Singh—both with heart conditions and solid records of backing Socialist policies to transform India's economy. But, with the IMF's guns trained on them, they performed the most comprehensive overhaul of India's economic policy regime in history. The old license-quota-permit raj was dismantled. Entrepreneurs were encouraged and the cosy cartels of Indian business faced competition for the first time in their lives from efficient global competitors.

Even if Narasimha Rao had done nothing else as Prime Minister, he will be remembered for his role in freeing the Indian economy. From 1991 onwards, India has faced the odd road bump or faltered at one or two hurdles but the broad direction of economic policy has been clear. All governments and all parties (except perhaps for the Left) now accept that the only way forward for the country is to unleash the entrepreneurial spirit of the Indian people.

But Rao did do one other thing and unfortunately for him, that may overshadow his other non-economic achievements. It was no secret in Delhi's political circles that Rao was considered to be soft on Hindutva. I doubt if he was communal or anti-Muslim and I don't think he subscribed at all to the RSS ideology. But equally, he was no hard secularist of the sort that the Congress was used to. At some level, he sympathised with Hindu revivalism.

Whether it was this sympathy or his own failures as a leader that led to the demolition of the Babri Masjid remains a matter of debate to this day. My own view is that his role during the demolition was not one of secret Hindutva lobbyist. It had more to do with the inability to take a decision.

What happened was this. During Narasimha Rao's tenure as Prime Minister, all his attempts to settle the Ayodhya dispute failed. L K Advani led the agitation to greater heights and on 6 December 1992, about a year and a half after Rao had become Prime Minister, the courts gave permission to hold the ceremony of kar seva (voluntary religious service) on the site of the mosque. The UP government, which was run by the BJP's Kalyan Singh, assured the courts that no damage would come to the structure.

On 6 December, around 1,50,000 kar sevaks gathered at the site and heard speeches by Uma Bharti, L K Advani and Dr Murli Manohar Joshi that inflamed their sentiments. At some stage, a young man broke through the police cordon and climbed on to the roof of the building. Seeing him on top of the dome, the crowd pushed the cordon and surrounded the mosque. Then, assorted kar sevaks also climbed on to the dome.

While all this was going on, two other things happened. One: the police force fled. And two, several journalists and cameramen were assaulted and driven away. So we have few independent, authentic accounts of what happened for the rest of the day. But cameras did record the beginning of the demolition of the mosque before the photographers were chased away.

As news that the masjid was being demolished reached Delhi, India looked to the Prime Minister. But Narasimha Rao did nothing. There was not a cheep out of the Prime Minister's Office till Kalyan Singh resigned as Chief Minister later that day. The kar sevaks stayed on for the entire night and even constructed a makeshift temple on the site where the Babri Masjid had stood.

Afterwards, Rao said he had been misled by Kalyan Singh who had promised to protect the mosque. Kalyan Singh was the man who had failed to stop the demolition. How could the Prime Minister be blamed?

With the luxury of 20/20 hindsight we now have a rough idea of what happened on 6 December 1992. An angry mob cannot demolish a large stone structure with its bare hands. Photos tell us that the men who pulled down the masjid had the implements required to destroy a building. They also had construction materials to build a makeshift temple.

So the demolition was not spontaneous. Somebody had clearly planned it. But who was this somebody? And how many people knew about the plan?

Everybody has their own view. But speaking for myself, I don't believe L K Advani knew. After the demolition began, the late Pramod Mahajan took Advani to a guest house. Later Mahajan told me that Advani was shattered and near tears. According to Mahajan, he said, 'They have destroyed my movement.'

So who did it? It was obviously a well-trained group within the sangh parivar. Clearly this group was well-connected to get its implements of destruction through the police cordon. Obviously, somebody in the UP administration also knew and helped them. Did the complicity go all the way to the top? Was Kalyan Singh involved? Honestly, I don't know. And no one has been able to prove that he was in on the plan.

Narasimha Rao's role comes in for attack on many grounds. First of all, should he have left it to UP's BJP government to protect the mosque? Shouldn't the Centre have sent forces? Secondly, should he have sat tight when the demolition was going on? His critics say his inaction proved he was happy to see the mosque go down. My view is that he simply funked it. We had seen examples of this. Rao was Home Minister in 1984 during the Delhi riots and just froze, refusing to take any action. My guess is that he did the same this time.

Not everyone agrees. The day after the demolition I asked Mani Shankar Aiyar, the former Rajiv-aide who was now an MP, why his Prime Minister seemed paralysed. 'Paralysed?' Aiyar retorted. 'He is not paralysed. Rigor mortis has set in.'

There are more sinister explanations for Rao's behaviour. Shahid Siddiqui believes that Rao wanted the Babri Masjid to be demolished: 'He thought he will be able to get rid of this issue once and for all and then get the credit for letting the mandir be built.'

It is a serious charge but Siddiqui sticks to it. He says that at the National Integration Council meeting held before the demolition, the BJP walked out because the consensus among all non-BJP participants was that the Kalyan Singh government should be dismissed because it could not be trusted to protect the Babri Masjid. A resolution was even passed to this effect. So Rao had the moral justification he needed to dismiss the government. But he did nothing.

Then, continues Siddiqui, 'Everyone knew that something terrible was going to happen. We had assembled at Suleman Sait's house on 6 December waiting to see what would happen. At 12:30 pm, we received the information that the first dome had fallen. We called up the PMO every fifteen minutes and the answer was always the same: "PM is resting."

'At 2:30 pm we went to meet President Shankar Dayal Sharma. He was in tears. And he showed us a letter he had written to the PM before the demolition asking him to dismiss the UP government. Then he told us that even he had not been able to get in touch with the PM. Narasimha Rao would not take the President of India's calls!'

According to Siddiqui, as the demolition proceeded, Rao went into seclusion refusing to take any calls. At 6:30 pm, he called a cabinet meeting. 'And he gave us, a group of Muslim leaders, time to see him also at 6.30 pm. Before the cabinet meeting he came to see us briefly. I told him. Now that it has been demolished, don't allow it to become a temple. Take it over. The CRPF is only one and a half kilometres from the site. Let them take control and then we can build both a mosque and a temple on the site. He said, "Okay, yes, yes."'

In fact, says Siddiqui, Rao allowed, 'the kar sevaks to stay all night and construct a temporary temple. And the CRPF jawans were asked to join the puja.'

Even if you believe that Rao was powerless to stop the demolition of the Babri Masjid, there is no doubt that he mishandled the aftermath. Riots broke out all over India as angry and betrayed Muslims took to the streets. But Rao failed to act quickly enough to stop the bloodshed. Worst of all and most unforgivable was his response to the Bombay riots of the next month, January 1993. As India's commercial capital burned, Rao sat back and did nothing. Later, much later, when 900 people had died, the army was sent in and order restored.

The consequence of all this was a long-term disaster for the Congress. The Muslims who had counted on the party for decades drifted away. They never came back. And to this day, the Congress has difficulty in persuading Muslims that it can safeguard their interests. In electoral terms that is Narasimha Rao's lasting legacy.

If the Babri Masjid demolition had happened in the twenty-first century on live TV and if TV crews had been attacked, the government would have fallen and the media would never have forgiven the BJP. But that was a different era with no private TV channels and no social media. So Rao survived. And the BJP escaped the ill-will of the entire media.

Only one man could have challenged him. Arjun Singh, his effective Number Two in the cabinet. But Singh failed to act and the opportunity was missed.

Meanwhile, Rao had another problem. Having turned down the prime ministership, Sonia Gandhi had refused to get into politics. She spent her time running the Rajiv Gandhi Foundation and followed the inquiry into her husband's assassination with obsessive attention. But Sonia felt that Rao had no interest in getting to the bottom of the case. He refused her requests for information, seemed to be going slow on the investigation and eventually began to rebuff her completely. I recall him once telling me angrily, 'What does that lady want? Whatever I do, she is never satisfied.'

And so the old Rajiv loyalists—Arjun Singh, N D Tiwari, Sheila Dixit, Natwar Singh and many others, formed their own version of the Congress. Though she said nothing publicly, it was apparent that Sonia Gandhi was on their side.

Looking back at the disasters that befell Narasimha Rao's minority government, it is a miracle that the Prime Minister survived. The Babri Masjid demolition, bloody riots, a Congress split—nothing seemed to phase him. He even brushed off public allegations made by Harshad Mehta, the stockbroker and principal protagonist in the stock scam, that he had personally delivered a suitcase containing a crore of rupees to Narasimha Rao in the Prime Minister's house.

The key to understanding Narasimha Rao, I wrote during that period, is that he is a small-time manipulator who masquerades as a statesman. Rao never really forgave me for that column. And in any case, I now concede I was wrong. He was not a small-time manipulator. He was a very big-time manipulator.

At the end of his term came what was either his final manipulation or, to believe Rao himself, his attempt to cleanse the system. A diary belonging to a Madhya Pradesh businessman called Surinder Jain had fallen into the hands of authorities. In this diary, Jain listed payments to people who were only identified by their initials. The investigators were hesitant to act on the basis of initials alone but were pushed into taking the case forward by Justice Verma of the Supreme Court who was overseeing the matter. They concluded that each initial corresponded to a prominent political figure. So K N was Kamal Nath. Y S was Yashwant Sinha, VCS was V C Shukla, MRS was Madhavrao Scindia and most significantly, that LKA was L K Advani.

Even a child could see that this was not enough to go on. To conclude that L K Advani had received money from Surinder Jain, you had to look at Advani's accounts, his pattern of spending etc., to see if there had been an unexplained inflow of funds. You needed to check whether Jain had met Advani on the dates mentioned in the diary to hand over any money. Mere initials were not enough.

But the CBI, egged on by the Court and supervised by Rao, did none of the above. Instead it filed criminal cases against all of those whose initials seemed to feature in the diary. This included many members of Rao's own cabinet who had to resign. It also meant that the CBI charged L K Advani with corruption. Advani alleged that he was being framed and declared that he would not seek election till his name had been cleared.

From Rao's point of view, the chargesheet was supposed to be a master stroke. He went into the 1996 election not as the man who took a crore from Harshad Mehta or the man under whose watch the Babri Masjid was demolished, but as the Prime Minister who was so eager to clean up the system that he did not even spare his own ministers. Moreover, Rao found new allies. He tied up with the Bahujan Samaj Party (BSP) for seat-sharing and gifted away some of the Congress' safest seats—seats where the Dalits had consistently voted for the Congress.

But when the results were declared, it was all for naught. The Congress slumped to its lowest ever total, winning 141 seats. And even though Rao tried to stay on in office, arguing that this was a hung parliament, nobody would support him. His own party was appalled. Not only had he lost them the Muslims, he had also lost them the Dalits. The BSP won the previously safe Congress' seats it had been gifted. And it was to hold on to the Dalits who never came back to the Congress. It would take the Congress another eight years to get into office again.

A new star was rising. And a new era was beginning. The era of Atal Bihari Vajpayee.

Chapter Six

The Vajpayee Era

Despite being a man with no political base, P V Narasimha Rao had survived the hatred of his colleagues by making deals and doing trades. So, when the results of the 1996 election began streaming in, Rao was not unduly worried. Yes, the Muslims, still shattered by the demolition of the Babri Masjid had turned to other parties. Yes, the Dalits had followed Rao's suggestion that they vote for the Bahujan Samaj Party. And yes, the middle class thought he was a ruthless crook.

But Rao knew that the results would throw up a hung parliament. And in that situation, it is always possible to negotiate a parliamentary majority or buy a coalition. What he had not reckoned with was the growing popularity of the BJP which ended up as the largest party in parliament with 161 seats whereas the Congress was reduced to 141. No matter, Rao was confident that as the BJP was a political untouchable, it would not get enough allies to reach the majority mark.

He was right. And he was wrong. While the BJP still had not reached the point of political lift-off, it had a trump card in the form of Atal Bihari Vajpayee who reclaimed the leadership from L K Advani. Even those who were not BJP supporters regarded Vajpayee as the only statesman in the political landscape. He was a moderate, was secular, had a modern worldview and commanded respect across the political spectrum.

But Vajpayee was a realist. He had joined the BJP recognising that the party would never come to power during his lifetime. That did not matter so much to him. He had never been after power. Otherwise, he would have accepted Narasimha Rao's offer, made in 1993, to join the Congress. He was happy sitting in the opposition and sticking to his principles.

Then, on 15 May 1996, the unthinkable happened. Vajpayee was summoned to Rashtrapati Bhavan by President Shankar Dayal Sharma and handed over a letter. As the BJP was the single largest party in the House, it got the first chance to form the government. Vajpayee would be Prime Minister. He had till 31 May to prove his majority. People who met him right afterwards say he had tears in his eyes. All of his life, he had worked for the party without ever imagining that this day would come. He knew, as did nearly everyone else, that he would not be able to cobble together a majority. But it was important to take office, to send out the message that the BJP could handle the responsibility of governance.

Thirteen days later, when the BJP came nowhere near a majority, Vajpayee resigned. But he did it in grand style. His final speech to parliament as Prime Minister was televised nationally and it was so electrifying that the whole country stopped what it was doing and turned on the TV. I wrote at the time that the speech proved that Vajpayee was prime ministerial material. This was not the end, I said. But the beginning.

Not everyone saw it that way of course. With Vajpayee gone, Narasimha Rao renewed his efforts to return to office. He was shocked when the so-called secular parties told him that he was now completely unacceptable to them. Instead, the secular alliances went back to V P Singh and asked him to take the job. (Despite their history, the Congress, under Rao, said it would support Singh as Prime Minister!) V P Singh, who had been burned once and was in poor health turned down the job. Then, they went to Jyoti Basu who was eager to become prime minister, but the politburo said no. The CPM would not join the government. A bitter Jyoti Basu called it a historic blunder.

Amar Singh, the veteran Indian strategist and fixer has his own version of what happened. He denies, first of all, that V P Singh did not want the job. And though V P Singh's contemporaries say that he turned down the offer made to him by the Third Front, Amar Singh claims that V P Singh was more than happy to become prime minister. It was Mulayam Singh Yadav (whose principal advisor Amar Singh was, in that era) who objected to V P Singh's candidature.

So, who did that leave? Eventually the secular front came up with a dead loss candidate. H D Deve Gowda, a journeyman-politician from Karnataka took the job to no great enthusiasm. His tenure as prime minister was eminently forgettable. He told me later that the reason he kept falling asleep during important meetings was because he had difficulty sleeping at night owing to the stress of the job.

But Deve Gowda had a winning strategy. He knew he was dependent on Congress support and calculated that if he used his power as Prime Minister to tame the Congress, he would be more secure. So he launched inquiries against assorted Congress leaders and the investigative agencies specifically targeted Narasimha Rao. Such was the pressure on Rao that he had to step down as Congress president.

Rao told me later that he had looked for a reasonable figure. He thought he had found one in Sitaram Kesri, an eighty-two-year-old Congressman to whom the term "sleazeball" was often applied, perhaps unjustifiably and unreasonably. According to Rao when he discussed making him interim Congress president, Kesri took off his cap and placed it at Rao's feet. 'I will do as you ask,' he told Rao.

Rao should have known better. Once Kesri put his cap back on, he turned viciously against Rao and sacked him even as leader of the Congress Parliamentary Party (CPP). Then he began to take on Deve Gowda.

But Deve Gowda was no pushover. He quickly put it about that he was investigating the murder of Kesri's doctor. There was no evidence against Kesri but an investigation might air some dirty linen.

There was only one way this could end. In April 1997, Kesri told the President that the Congress was withdrawing support to Deve Gowda. He called leaders of the secular front and said enough was enough. Deve Gowda had to go. They agreed. But they were taken aback when Kesri announced who the next prime minister would be. It would be Kesri himself. The old buffer was dying to grab his Pomeranians and rush in to Race Course Road.

The Left vetoed the proposal. The secular front would continue, it said. But it would have a non-Congress prime minister. G K Moopanar of the Tamil Maanila Congress was a strong candidate but Harkishan Singh Surjeet, the chief wheeler-dealer within the CPM said he wanted Mulayam Singh Yadav.

Political journalist and secular activist, Kuldip Nayar had known Surjeet for years. He says that when he heard that Mulayam was going to be the prime ministerial candidate, he was shocked. Nayar went off to see Surjeet and said, 'Do you know that during his time people have been bumped off?' According to Nayar, Surjeet was surprised by the charge and turned to the younger CPM leader, Sitaram Yechuri who was also present. When Yechuri confirmed what Nayar had said, Surjeet began to reconsider.

Amar Singh agrees broadly with this version. He says that Surjeet had assured Mulayam that he would be the next prime minister and Mulayam had even called a photographer over to take his official portrait. Amar Singh admits that the Left changed its mind about Mulayam because it had heard about some of his criminal activities.

The difference between Amar Singh and Kuldip Nayar's versions is that according to Singh it was Jyoti Basu who changed the party's stance whereas Nayar says it was Surjeet.

Either way with Mulayam ruled out, the search for an acceptable prime minister continued. By now Surjeet had left for Moscow so the Left had less of a say. Even so, says Kuldip Nayar, he told I K Gujral, whom he was backing, to go and meet Jyoti Basu.

By the time the Third Front met at Andhra Bhavan to find a new prime minister, Gujral was a serious candidate. He was asked to join the meeting but when he realised that his was one of the names under discussion, he withdrew from the deliberations. Chandrababu Naidu had a bedroom at Andhra Bhavan opened and Gujral went to sleep.

At three in the morning they woke him up and told him he was the new Prime Minister of India.

He sat with Naidu and the others working out the mechanics of the accession and finally got home at six. His wife, who had been worried about his lengthy absence asked where he had gone and why it had taken so long?

Gujral was in a good mood. And so, he laughed and said to her, 'Hold your tongue. You are now talking to the Prime Minister of India!'

Inder Kumar Gujral was probably one of the most decent men to occupy the Prime Minister's Office. But there was not much he could do. Tormented by the Congress and belittled by members of his own cabinet, Gujral did his best till one of those bogus issues that taint Indian politics so often exploded.

The M C Jain Commission was investigating Rajiv Gandhi's assassination. In 1997, it issued an interim report suggesting that some of those who may have been involved in the assassination conspiracy may have had links with the Dravida Munnetra Kazhagam or DMK. This was only an interim report and when Jain eventually submitted his final report, he conceded that there were no DMK links.

But first Arjun Singh and then Sitaram Kesri hammered away at this issue. They would not support Gujral, they said, unless he sacked all DMK ministers from his government. To his credit, Gujral refused. And so, the Congress withdrew support.

Once again, Kesri made an abortive attempt to smuggle himself and his Pomeranians into Race Course Road. And once again, nobody would back the Congress. And so, less than two years after Narasimha Rao had been defeated, a new general election was called.

Inder Gujral was not a mass politician. Kesri was a nobody. And so the star of the 1997 election campaign was A B Vajpayee. His own campaign covered over 120 constituencies and with each speech he began to sound more and more like a prime minister. The country was now fed up with the so-called secular front, revolted by the likes of Narasimha Rao and Sitaram Kesri and wanted a firm, stable government. L K Advani had opted out of the 1996 election after being framed by Narasimha Rao in the Jain hawala case. Now, the cases had thrown out the charges and his promise not to stand for election till he was exonerated was no longer valid. But he recognised that this was Vajpayee's election. Advani was now Vajpayee's Number Two again.

When the results came on 4 March, the BJP and its allies had achieved the near impossible. The two years of Third Front shenanigans had so annoyed the people of India that they rewarded Vajpayee with another 80 seats over the 161 the BJP had won last time. With 264 seats, the BJP was within striking distance of a majority. Once the Telugu Desam Party's (TDP) Chandrababu Naidu indicated that he would not vote against the BJP, the path was clear. On 19 March 1998, Atal Bihari Vajpayee was sworn in as Prime Minister of India. This time, it was clear, he would stay for longer than thirteen days.

Throughout its time in opposition, the BJP had said that India would test nuclear weapons as soon as the party was in power. Nobody took this very seriously. But Vajpayee had meant every word of it. On 11 May, having successfully fooled the CIA which, despite its spy satellites had no idea of what was going on, India exploded two nuclear devices. Two days later, it exploded three more. The message was clear. This was a new government and it would not be business as usual.

When Pakistan retaliated by exploding its own devices on 28 May, the international community grew agitated. The region had now become "nuclear". There was talk of a need for international mediation to solve the Kashmir issue. It looked as though the tests, though widely welcomed within India, may have backfired by drawing world powers to the region.

So Vajpayee decided that the time was right for bilateral negotiations with Pakistan. After weeks of furious back-channel diplomacy, he declared that he would cross the Wagah border and go to Lahore by bus. He would hold talks with Pakistan's President, Nawaz Sharif in Lahore and India and Pakistan would work towards resolving their differences bilaterally.

G Parthasarathy was India's High Commissioner to Pakistan during that period. He thinks that the trip was a success on the whole but he has his doubts about the need for the theatricality of a bus-ride which led to increased expectations. In foreign policy terms however, Parthasarathy is clear that India had no choice. 'After the tests, India was subject to sanctions. A UN Security Council Resolution had been passed calling for UN intervention in Jammu and Kashmir,' he remembers. 'It was Resolution 13725, if I recall it correctly. So we had to make a meaningful gesture. And the trip established Mr. Vajpayee as a statesman willing to even reach out to someone who had been making jingoistic noises about nuclear weapons.'

The Lahore bus trip went well. But on the domestic front, Vajpayee's problems were mounting. Food inflation raged unchecked and dissatisfaction with the new government grew to the extent that the BJP lost assembly elections in three of the strongholds where it had done well in the parliamentary polls: Rajasthan, Madhya Pradesh and Delhi.

And then there were problems with its allies. Well, one ally in particular. Almost from the time that the BJP had taken office, J Jayalalithaa, the imperious leader of the All India Anna Dravida Munnetra Kazhagam or AIADMK had made impossible demands. She wanted old cases against her withdrawn; income tax officers transferred; Tamil Nadu's DMK state government dismissed. And so on. At first, Vajpayee tried to mollify her. But eventually her demands became so unreasonable that no government could agree to even meet her halfway. She wanted George Fernandes, the then Defence Minister fired. She wanted the dismissed Naval Chief re-instated. She wanted a Joint Parliamentary Committee or JPC set up. And so on. When Vajpayee refused to listen, Jayalalithaa opened a channel of communication to Sonia Gandhi who had taken over as Congress President. She told Sonia that she was preparing to bring Vajpayee down and would now back the Congress. She also sent emissaries to Harkishan Singh Surjeet, the veteran CPM leader, and asked him to construct yet another secular front.

Why did Sonia Gandhi go along with this? She must have known that for all the fake smiles, Jayalalithaa hated her. She must have also known that with the Congress' record of bringing down Gujral and Deve Gowda, another parliamentary coup would do no good. On the other hand, the Congress was on a roll. It had won three assembly elections. Opinion polls showed that Vajpayee's popularity was sinking. And Congress leaders told Sonia she would never get another chance like this.

So, in April 1999, J Jayalalithaa withdrew support. Vajpayee thought he could still make it. He was assured by Mayawati that she would support him. A confidence vote was called and on that very morning, Mayawati went to see Vajpayee, touched his feet, and assured him of the BSP's support. Then, her MPs went into the Lok Sabha and voted against the government. Vajapyee was defeated by just one vote. Mayawati was delighted. She told the press: 'I deliberately set out to fool the BJP.'

The onus now fell on Sonia Gandhi to construct an alternative coalition with the help of Surjeet. All seemed to be going well. She was promised support. She even went off to Rashtrapati Bhavan to tell the President that the Congress had the numbers. Then suddenly, it all went wrong. Mulayam Singh Yadav and Amar Singh declared that while they wanted Vajpayee out, they would not support a Congress-led coalition. It had to be a Third Front government. Jyoti Basu could be prime minister. They suggested Basu's name because they knew, from previous experience, that the politburo would not allow him to take the job. When this happened, they said, well... what about Mulayam for prime minister, then?

Mulayam was now so desperate to be prime minister that rather like Charan Singh in 1979, he was willing to do a deal with the enemy. A secret meeting was arranged between Mulayam and Amar Singh on the one side and the BJP's L K Advani on the other side. They met at Jaya Jaitley's house and Mulayam tried to get the BJP to support him for prime minister. Advani refused. But Mulayam promised that no matter what happened he would not allow the Congress to come to power. It had to be a Third Front ministry.

The Congress said a point-blank no to any Third Front government. So the President dissolved Parliament and called for yet another election in 1999—the third since 1996.

The Congress thought it had a good chance of winning. After all, the assembly elections had been going in its favour. But Kargil changed everything.

What actually happened in Kargil is a tricky subject and everyone has their own views. What we know for certain is that Pakistani forces occupied bunkers in vast areas of land belonging to India. The Indian army had abandoned the bunkers in the winter and took months to notice that the Pakistanis had moved in.

G Parthasarathy remembers that when he came to Delhi to take instructions from the government, he 'found huge arguments about who should take the rap. Whether it was the Intelligence Bureau, the R&AW or the military intelligence. Clearly, there was an intelligence failure. Because the Pakistanis had, in the winter months, seized all the great heights.'

The Intelligence Bureau's position is that it did know and that it had warned the army. Ajit Doval was a senior officer in IB and he says that a 'communication went from IB signed by the Director, IB. And normally, the IB chief does not sign any intelligence report. It said that there was going to be an intrusion and this is what is being planned. The army later said that because the communication was marked to the Army Chief and the DG Military Intelligence and not the DG Military Operations, no action could be taken. It was not a very convincing explanation.'

Within India, this was seen as a betrayal of the Lahore spirit. The Vajpayee government suggested that the occupation was an independent enterprise conducted by the Pakistan army without the knowledge of Nawaz Sharif, the peacemaker of Lahore.

G Parthasarathy who had actually been in Pakistan in the way up to the invasion disputes this. According to him, Nawaz Sharif was briefed about the operation by the army in October. 'Therefore, he knew about it even before the snowing began. He actually visited Skardo, the location of the force commander of the northern region who was actually in charge of the operation. We got reports that Sharif had said he was thrilled he could see the lights of Srinagar from the peaks over there. So yes, he knew about it and he was involved.'

No matter who set up Kargil or whether there was an intelligence failure, of one thing there is no doubt. The Indian army excelled itself in winning back our territory. Officers led from the front and sacrificed their lives. Often there was brutal hand to hand combat. But at the end of the day, India won. The infiltrators were beaten back. US President Bill Clinton responded to a call for help from Nawaz Sharif and a cease-fire was agreed to. Pakistan took the line that its army had never been involved. These were just mujahideen! And Sharif told India that the army did it without his knowledge.

Few countries vote against a prime minister who has just won a war. And so when India went to the polls in September and October 1999, Vajpayee was the clear favourite. And when the results were declared, the Congress found it had been pushed to a historic low of 114.The BJP had 182. And the NDA had 296, a comfortable majority.

It turned out that J Jayalalithaa may actually have done Vajpayee a favour.

It is probably a little early to judge Vajpayee. We will have to wait for the verdict of history for that. But some things stand out. First of all, he gave India stability and confidence. Those factors resulted in a huge economic boom. Secondly, he made the BJP electable. Till then it had been seen as a party of small shopkeepers, masjid-breakers and Muslim-haters. Vajpayee proved that the BJP was much more than that. Thirdly, with the help of his brilliant Principal Secretary, Brajesh Mishra, he re-oriented Indian foreign policy, improved relations with America which he called India's natural ally and even restored some normalcy to our ties with Pakistan.

But not everything went perfectly. There was the fiasco of IC 814, for instance. This was an Indian Airlines plane, hijacked by Pakistani terrorists on a scheduled flight from Kathmandu to Delhi. When the plane landed at Amritsar to refuel, it should have been stopped. But the government reacted too late and the plane flew off. Eventually, India released three terrorists from jail to save the lives of the passengers. As humiliating as this was, what was worse was that the Foreign Minister, Jaswant Singh actually escorted the terrorists to Kandahar, in Afghanistan.

Jaswant intended for the media to record this moment of shame. Ashok Tandon, Vajpayee's Media Advisor says 'I got a call from a journalist who was at the technical area of Delhi airport that a press party was going to Kandahar. I was shocked. My first thought was that I had to stop the press party from going. But I did not have the authority to do it.'

So Tandon called Vajpayee's residence. He was told that the Prime Minister had just finished lunch and was resting in his room. A desperate Tandon then asked to speak to Namita Bhattacharya, Vajpayee's foster daughter. 'I told Namita that I know you don't interfere in government. But I am desperate and I need your help. Please disturb the boss. We have to stop this.'

And so Vajpayee made sure the press party remained on the tarmac.

Then, there was the attack on parliament. This was both an intelligence and security failure. By the time the terrorists were stopped, many Indian police personnel had died. And the terrorists came perilously close to taking MPs hostage and blowing up parts of the building. India's response, a huge military operation on the Pakistan border, Operation Parakram, cost thousands of crores of rupees and achieved nothing.

And finally, there were the Gujarat riots which remain controversial to this day. What happened was this: on 27 February 2002, a mob set fire to a train carrying kar sevaks returning from Ayodhya. Fifty-nine people, including twenty-five women and fifteen children were burnt to death. The victims were Hindus. The mob was Muslim.

Some reaction was inevitable because Gujarat has always been such a tinderbox of communal passion that any spark can light a fire. So inevitably, riots broke out in Ahmedabad and other cities. What was most horrifying though was that the police failed to protect Muslim victims of violence. And the savagery exhibited by Hindu mobs was without precedent.

The controversy surrounds the role played by the then Chief Minister, Narendra Modi, who had only just taken over. One view is that he instructed the police to let Hindus attack Muslims. After all, kar sevaks had been burnt alive in Godhra and unless the BJP let Hindus express their anger, it would alienate its political base.

While this view is still current among Modi's detractors, the fact remains that over a decade later, nobody has found any evidence that Modi asked the police to give the Hindu mobs a free rein or to prevent them from protecting Muslims.

A second view is that Modi was too new and inexperienced to handle such a complicated situation. According to this view, Modi's fault lies in refusing to heal the wounds caused by riots and by continuing to play the Hindu card. It does not help his case that sangh parivar leaders were clearly involved in the murder and the mayhem.

Whatever you believe, what we do know is that Vajpayee wanted to sack Modi. He spoke about the need for *insaniyat* (humanity) and went to the BJP's National Executive meeting in Goa determined to remove the chief minister. But Modi took the pre-emptive step of offering to resign. And then BJP leaders such as, Pramod Mahajan spoke up in Modi's defence. Faced with this revolt, Vajpayee backed down and Modi stayed. Ironically, among those who argued strongly on behalf of Modi was L K Advani. It was to prove to be the political equivalent of a turkey voting for an early Christmas.

There was one other notable failure in Vajpayee's term. Suddenly and without any preparation, the government reversed its position on not talking to Pakistan and invited the country's military dictator to Agra for a summit. The meeting ended in a statement and nothing was achieved.

G Parthasarathy is convinced that the Agra summit was a mistake. 'If you are having a summit, you need detailed preparations and talks so that everything is decided beforehand and all you have to do is sign the final communique. That is what happened in Lahore. But here, we invited Musharraf without any preparations. More important, we invited him within two months of a terrorist attack on the Red Fort.'

But overall, Vajpayee had a good run. He showed us a softer, gentler BJP, one where no communal agenda influenced the government in Delhi and one where the RSS did not call the shots. He won a war with Pakistan, he turned India into a nuclear power and he gained the world's respect. He was a middle class hero, a statesman in the mould of Jawaharlal Nehru.

Every opinion poll in 2004 suggested he was coming back with a huge majority and the government was so confident that it advanced the election. Even the Congress did not think it was going to win.

But when the results were declared, the people of India had told the media and the political class how little we know. The opinion polls were wrong, the journalists were wrong and the politicians were wrong. The BJP was defeated. The Vajpayee era was over. And India was set for a decade of Congress rule.

Chapter Seven

Cutting A Deal

In 2004, India was doing extraordinarily well. The middle class had begun to look to the West for its reference points. Foreign companies rushed to invest in the economy. Commentators removed the old hyphenation of India-Pakistan and began a new one: India-China. The BJP government of A B Vajpayee seemed popular and a new ad campaign captured the spirit of optimism. India Shining, it bragged.

The media and the opinion polls reflected this euphoria. Almost every poll predicted an overall majority for the BJP if an election were to be called and the party agreed with this assessment. It regarded the Congress as a useless and fragmented opposition led by a woman who Vajpayee had already defeated twice at the polls and who did not have the confidence of her own party.

Sonia Gandhi had finally entered politics in 1998. She had done so, first as a campaigner, when the party then led by Sitaram Kesri, seemed about to be consigned to the dustbin of history. Then after the BJP had trashed the Congress, the party had sacked Kesri and Sonia, overturning the publicly-stated reluctance of a lifetime, had agreed to be party president.

Why had she changed her mind? In an interview a few years after she took the plunge, she gave me her reasons: 'In 1998 the Congress party was going through a deep crisis. Elections were declared. And some of our people moved to the BJP. Many Congress people had come to plead with me to at least go out and campaign for the party. I felt that it would be very cowardly to just sit here and watch the party go through this bad phase.'

But, of course, she did more than campaign. A little later she joined politics and became party president—the very same job she had turned down in 1991. So why did she agree to accept the post eight years later?

'I did that because I had lived in a family which had lived and died, practically, for the country and for the Congress party. I felt it was my duty to my family to just lend a supporting hand.'

Later, she added, 'I could not have walked passed the pictures and portraits of my husband, of my mother-in-law and of Panditji that hang on these walls unless I felt I had done something to help the Congress at the time of its greatest crisis.'

In fact, there seemed to be no evidence that she could turn the fortunes of the party around. She collaborated with J Jayalalithaa of the AIADMK to bring down the Vajpayee government only to face a terrible defeat in the election that followed.

Her colleagues were of the view that the Congress had played the Sonia card and that it had failed. There was nothing more to be gained by soldiering on under her leadership. After conspiring for weeks, Sharad Pawar went public with his reservations. He was joined by Purno Sangma, the former Speaker and Tariq Anwar, a Bihar politician. It was rumoured that several other Congressmen were ready to join the revolt once it looked as though it might succeed.

Pawar and Sangma openly raised the issue of Sonia's foreign birth. Should the Congress be led by a person born in Italy? Sonia reacted emotionally. She announced she would resign as Congress President. She was a reluctant politician anyway. And if the Congress did not want her, well then it could find somebody else.

I asked Sonia how she felt when the revolt began. 'I was certainly taken aback,' she said. 'Because first of all this was an issue which the opposition had taken up. But more so because when they had come and asked me to participate in the election campaign and later to become President of the Congress party, this issue never crossed their minds. This issue did not feature at all.'

Her emotional response united the rank and file of the Congress cadres who demanded that she withdraw her resignation. And senior Congressmen spoke up in her favour. Dr Manmohan Singh once told me, in a TV interview, that 'the dissidents had been part of the decision taken to make Soniaji the Congress President.' In fact, he added, 'Sharad Pawar was a party along with me. He moved the resolution to make Shrimati Sonia Gandhi Chairperson of the Congress Parliamentary Party. I seconded it. When the Vajpayee government fell, all of them (the dissidents) voted for a resolution asking the President to invite Shrimati Sonia Gandhi to explore the opportunities of forming an alternative government.'

Eventually, the revolt ran out of steam. Those who had sat on the fence decided eventually to back Sonia and she withdrew her resignation. Pawar and his colleagues left to form the Nationalist Congress Party or NCP.

And the Congress stuck by Sonia. Though all through the glory days of the Vajpayee government, the Congress kept a low profile, not doing particularly well in assembly elections and maintaining a restrained parliamentary presence.

So when the BJP saw the results of opinion polls that predicted a two-thirds majority, it was so delighted, it even advanced the election by a few months. India was shining and so would the election results.

During the campaign however, Sonia Gandhi began to find that the mood in the villages of India did not mirror the middle class euphoria of the cities. The rural poor had not benefitted from liberalisation. Farmers, crushed by the burden of debt, were committing suicide. Muslims felt further alienated after the 2002 Gujarat riots. Some were even ready to forgive the Congress for the demolition of the Babri Masjid and the soft Hindutva of the Narasimha Rao years and to return to the fold.

The BJP saw none of this. Till the very end it remained confident of victory. When the exit polls, while still giving victory to the BJP, suggested that the Congress was faring better than had been previously predicted, the BJP dismissed the findings. Even within the Congress, the mood was sombre. The best the party could hope for was a Third Front government, or so it believed.

But when the results began streaming in, the pollsters were left red-faced. The BJP had slumped from 182 seats to 138 seats. The Congress had risen from 114 to 145 seats. If it got the support of a few allies, then there was no problem: the Congress would form the next government. A delighted but still strangely thoughtful Sonia set about putting her coalition in place. The Left jumped on board. So did many allies. Even Sharad Pawar's NCP said it would now support her as prime minister leading people to wonder why Pawar and his friends had needed to split the party to begin with.

When the coalition was in place and the Congress was ready to take office, Sonia pulled a surprise. She issued a statement in which she said she had listened to her inner voice and decided that she would not be prime minister. The statement, drafted for her by her daughter Priyanka, confirmed what friends of the family had long suspected: Sonia never had any intention of becoming prime minister. Partly it was that she recognised that the foreigner issue would never go away. Partly it was that her children having seen their grandmother and father assassinated did not want another member of the family to take the job. And partly it was that she genuinely felt that she lacked any experience of government.

What follows next is speculation. But two different sources told me that when Sonia went to see President K R Narayanan in 1999 during the turmoil that followed Vajpayee's defeat in the confidence vote, she told him that she did not wish to be prime minister. One source, R D Pradhan, who was her principal aide at the time, was clear: even in 1999, she did not want the job. My second source was President K R Narayanan who told me that she had asked him to swear Manmohan Singh in once the coalition had gathered the numbers. Of course, that never happened.

Did Manmohan Singh know this? Opinions are divided and the man himself is decidedly shifty on the subject. There's no doubt he was dying to become prime minister. In 1997, when Deve Gowda's government tottered, he had gently put it about that he was available for the job. I'd asked him if he wanted to be prime minister and he had replied. 'Who doesn't want to be PM?' To his credit, when he did become Prime Minister in 2004, he reminded me of that conversation.

My guess is that Sonia told him in 1999 that he was her choice. And after that, when he knew that the job was within his reach—even if things had not worked out in 1999—he decided to play it cool. A year later, when I asked him about it, this time on TV, he was evasive. 'Well, Mrs Gandhi has said that the party will take the decision,' he said.

Five years later, when the Congress had beaten the odds and made it to office, Sonia turned to Manmohan once again. This time he was ready. I remember watching him go to 10 Janpath, eyes gleaming with excitement, hands trembling with anticipation, eager to become Sonia's nominee for the job.

But the Congress was not ready. Congressmen and women wept and begged Sonia to reconsider. She refused point-blank. Manmohan Singh was her choice, she said, and she would not be swayed.

What Sonia Gandhi was proposing was unprecedented. She wanted an arrangement whereby she would continue as Congress President and would handle relations with the allies, an important component of the running of any coalition. Manmohan Singh, on the other hand, would have a free hand when it came to the government.

There were many ways of looking at this arrangement. You could see it as Sonia's attempt to sidestep the foreign origin issue and exercise power without formal accountability to parliament. And indeed that is how her critics saw it.

Or you could see it as an extraordinarily selfless gesture, which is how her fans saw it. Few people willingly turn down the prime ministership of the world's largest democracy.

But what nobody could deny was that it was going to be difficult to make the arrangement work. There were just too many problems.

The first was the party. Put simply, nobody in the Congress had any enthusiasm for a Manmohan Singh prime ministership. He was not well-liked, was seen as a creation of the hated Narasimha Rao and hardcore politicians had contempt for his lack of political skills. He had only ever stood for election to the Lok Sabha once. And he'd been soundly defeated. This was a mandate for Sonia Gandhi, they said, not for some time serving bureaucrat-turned-politician.

The second problem was with the allies. Some, like Laloo Yadav, had to be persuaded to accept Manmohan Singh as prime minister. The Left was downright hostile. They saw Singh as a creation of the World Bank-American lobby, as a stooge of the West who had no feel for India's poor and insufficient concern for India's sovereignty.

But Manmohan Singh had his admirers. Most people who did not know him well regarded him as a humble, decent, apolitical figure who had no great ambition. And certainly there was much to admire. He was a towering intellect, a first rate economist and a man of such scrupulous honesty that throughout his career he had refused to even let his family use his official car. Many in the middle class saw him as the father of India's liberalisation and believed that he would now completely unshackle the economy.

So when Manmohan Singh took office, the general reaction was overwhelmingly favourable. A new liberal, secular and inclusive era had dawned.

Though we did not see it then, it seems clear in retrospect, that the seeds for the fall of the United Progressive Alliance or UPA were sown in the very first years of the government. The first was the ideological divide. Sonia Gandhi was, at heart, what was sometimes disparagingly referred to as a *jholawali* or bleeding-heart NGO-typc. Her travels throughout India during the election campaign had convinced her that the benefits of liberalisation had not been equally shared and that they had not penetrated to the very bottom of Indian society.

She believed that the formal economy and the market were inadequate mechanisms to benefit the poor. She wanted direct transfers of wealth to those at the very bottom of the class structure.

Manmohan Singh, on the other hand, had spent his life working within the formal economy. He was not prepared to endorse a regime of subsidies, welfare schemes and direct transfers. His formula was to encourage the West to invest and to then wait for the fruits of globalisation to reach the poor.

Because she lacked the formal economic training to combat Manmohan Singh's intellect, Sonia Gandhi set up her own private think tank called the National Advisory Council or NAC and filled it with NGO-type and *jholawallas* like herself. Manmohan Singh had scant respect for the NAC and his officials had contempt for many of its recommendations, a view that was frequently expressed in off-the-record briefing to the media and became the standard position of the pink papers.

In the first year of the government, Sonia and the NAC pushed through many schemes for which Manmohan Singh had no real enthusiasm. She insisted on a write-off on farmers' loan. She had seen too many farmers commit suicide because of debt, she said. And it was wrong for the middle class to prosper while the poor drank pesticide and killed themselves. She introduced an employment-guarantee scheme based loosely on a model that had worked in Maharashtra. And she forced a reluctant Manmohan Singh to accept the principle of a Right To Information (RTI) Act.

Nearly all of these proposals came from the NAC which the Prime Minister and his men continued to view with suspicion. But who were the Prime Minister's Men? In Vajpayee's days, the all-powerful Brajesh Mishra had been both Principal Secretary and National Security Advisor. Even when the Subramaniam Committee set up to look at the Kargil debacle had recommended splitting the job, Vajpayee had refused to do so. Now, Manmohan Singh said he wanted a separate National Security Advisor. Sonia agreed and there was no dispute on the choice: J N aka Mani Dixit, one of India's finest former foreign secretaries. Neither Sonia nor Manmohan got their first choice as Principal Secretary. Manmohan wanted N N Vohra, a veteran civil servant with a great reputation. But Vohra turned down the job. Sonia wanted R Vasudevan, a widely respected former bureaucrat, who had been part of Rajiv Gandhi's PMO. But he too turned down the job. Finally, Manmohan Singh appointed a little-known man called T K A Nair on the grounds that he was comfortable with somebody from the Punjab cadre of the IAS.

Manmohan Singh wanted an Internal Security Advisor and suggested the name of M K Narayanan who had been close to Rajiv Gandhi as Director of the Intelligence Bureau. Sonia resented Narayanan who, she believed, had failed, when he served under V P Singh, to provide adequate security to Rajiv Gandhi. Eventually, she came around and Narayanan said he would divide his time between Chennai and Delhi and spend three days in the PMO.

Manmohan Singh asked for Sanjaya Baru, editor of the *Financial Express,* and a widely respected journalist to be his Media Advisor and Sonia agreed with his choice. He had always depended on Montek Singh Ahluwalia who had been Secretary in the finance ministry when the reforms were introduced. Ahluwalia had also been part of Rajiv's PMO so Sonia knew him and was pleased with his appointment as deputy chairman of the Planning Commission.

So what could go wrong?

Well, for a start there was the foreign policy quagmire. Early in his term, Manmohan Singh told his aides that apart from the economy—which was doing well anyway—his real priority was foreign policy. He wanted first to make peace with Pakistan and then, to move closer to the US.

It all began well with Foreign Minister Natwar Singh a willing participant. But then, Mani Dixit suddenly died. Singh was urged to find somebody with foreign policy experience to replace him. Instead, he chose to go with Narayanan. Nobody disputed that Narayanan was a first rate intelligence officer. But there was nothing in his record to suggest that he had any understanding of foreign policy. Singh appointed him to replace Dixit anyway.

Manmohan Singh's great obsession was Pakistan. He was determined to resolve the Kashmir dispute during his term. He persisted with this agenda despite the scepticism of first, Dixit who had served as ambassador to Pakistan and knew the country well and then, Narayanan who was as leery about Pakistan's intentions as Dixit had been. But Singh would not be swayed. And several times he told Congressmen that he was near a breakthrough.

Manmohan Singh's defenders say that his parleys with Gen. Parvez Musharraf, nearly led to a solution of the Kashmir dispute according to a formula worked out by the two leaders. Others say that neither Musharraf nor Singh could ever have sold this so-called settlement to the people of their own countries.

What the settlement entailed has never been officially confirmed. Those in the know say that there were several components. One, both sides would agree to treat the ceasefire line as the international border. Two, this Kashmir border would be "soft" which is to say that Kashmiris would find it easy to come and go from Pakistan-occupied Kashmir to the Indian part. Trade between the two countries would also have been liberalised. And three, India would massively or at least, significantly, scale down its military presence in Kashmir.

It is easy to see what India had to gain from a resolution of the Kashmir dispute that effectively sanctified the current territorial borders and ended Pakistan's interference in the state. But what did Pakistan gain by giving up its claim to Kashmir? Could Musharraf have found support for this position within Pakistan? Would Indian politicians have agreed to Pakistanis freely crossing the border? Would they have supported a reduction in the military presence in the Valley?

Whichever view you inclined to, what is certain is that nothing came of these discussions. Musharraf was overthrown and the newly-elected government of Nawaz Sharif refused to go along with what had allegedly been agreed.

That left Singh with his US agenda. Early in his prime ministership he had been bowled over by the warmth extended to him by President George W Bush and was pleased when Bush told him that the US would agree to a deal that allowed India access to nuclear material for energy generation. This was a significant breakthrough and an end to the nuclear apartheid that had persisted for decades. Singh hailed this as a triumph for his foreign policy even though there were dissenters within the UPA and outside. The Samajwadi Party bitterly opposed the deal. So did the Left.

Of the two, the Left was the real problem. The Communist partners had never liked Singh nor approved of his globalisation agenda though, to be fair, they were not against liberalisation within India. Singh had more or less given up on CPM supremo, Prakash Karat who had blocked his plans to increase limits for foreign investment in many sectors.

From Singh's perspective, the Left had destroyed both his agendas. He could not attract more foreign investment to get the economy moving as long as the Left maintained its rigid stance. And he couldn't move closer to America without the nuclear deal.

He was therefore bitterly disappointed when Sonia Gandhi declared that though she approved of the nuclear deal, she did not think it was worth sacrificing the government over. Because, if the deal went ahead, the Left would almost certainly withdraw support and the government would fall.

While Singh was stewing over the failure of the Left to support the nuclear deal, another crisis was brewing.

Terrorists were sent from Pakistan to attack the crucial city of Mumbai. We still cannot be sure how many terrorists there were or whether they had local support. But we do know that they exposed first, the government's naïveté in believing that the Pakistani establishment wanted peace and second, the weakness of our security set-up.

India had advance warning of the attacks from a variety of sources: interrogations, tip-offs from the CIA and RA&W's own intercepts of conversations between the terrorists and their Pakistani handlers. But still, the intelligence apparatus failed to take action. And when the attacks took place, we reacted with confusion and delay causing several deaths.

After the terrorists were overpowered or killed, one man, Ajmal Kasab survived. He told a terrifying story of Pakistani complicity at the highest levels. Whatever peace initiative Manmohan Singh had attempted had clearly failed.

But Dr Manmohan Singh stuck by his people. In the aftermath of the attacks, the Home Minister of India and the Chief Minister and Deputy Chief Minister of Maharashtra all lost their jobs. But Singh first agreed to sack M K Narayanan, the Intelligence czar and then backtracked, delaying removing him and offering excuses to Sonia Gandhi and the Congress' core group which had demanded his dismissal.

If the Pakistan agenda had failed, then would America be a flop as well, Singh was determined to make sure that on that score, at least, he would deliver. He told Sonia Gandhi he would resign unless the nuclear deal went ahead.

This was easier said than done. The Left would withdraw support. So how was the government to survive? Singh produced his old friend, Amar Singh of the Samajwadi Party and said the SP would now back the deal.

The Samajwadi turnaround has long been a subject of speculation in political circles. Sanjaya Baru, who was one of the early go-betweens thinks that it is not difficult to work out why the Samajwadi Party changed its position on the deal.

Says Dr Baru, 'It was just so obvious to me that once the Samajwadi Party lost power in UP, they were left without office. And this was an excellent opportunity to return to office in Delhi.'

According to Baru, Mulayam and Amar Singh hoped that if they supported the nuclear deal, Manmohan Singh would invite the SP to join the government and they would get important ministerial posts. And Manmohan Singh may well have been willing to agree to these terms.

Others say it was more complicated than that. Shahid Siddiqui was the official spokesman for the SP and had done the round of TV channels tearing into the deal when he was told that the party had changed its mind. 'I have not been able to work out what happened. But whatever happened was very sleazy. I suddenly received a call from Amar Singh that we are now supporting the deal.' Siddiqui was told that the SP now believed that the deal was in the national interest. 'I asked him to please explain to me how the deal is in the national interest. I can convince you that it is not in the national interest. And he had no explanation.

Suddenly they had changed to the extent that they were ready to do anything, go to any lengths to save the Manmohan Singh government.'

I asked Amar Singh why the SP had changed its mind. He said that somebody met him in Colorado when he had gone to America for medical treatment and persuaded him to support this deal.

And who was this "somebody"? 'That I will never tell,' said Amar Singh mysteriously. 'It is better that I remain quiet.'

And what were the reasons for this change of heart? Why did he suddenly decide that the deal was in the national interest?

'There was a solid reason for our change in attitude towards the Congress at that point in time,' said Amar. 'The reasons were not ideological or nationalistic. They were very personal.'

No matter what these reasons were, the fact remained that with the Left committed to opposing the deal, the UPA did not have a majority even with the SP's support. So how did Manmohan Singh hope to win the vote? Did he expect his party to buy him a majority?

The BJP says he did and claims that there was a cash-for-votes scam. Anyhow, the UPA won and the deal was passed. But the SP got no share of power.

'After the vote was over,' says Sanjaya Baru, 'there is this famous visual which was on TV when Amar Singh and Mulayam go to 7 RCR (PM House), they have a meeting with the PM and when they come out, they look livid. My guess is that Manmohan Singh had said to them: sorry,

I cannot take you in the government. I think part of the reason was this whole cash-for-votes scam.'

When the 2009 election was called, the pollsters said that the BJP would win. Eager ministerial aspirants asked L K Advani who was certain to be the BJP's choice for prime minister to allot portfolios to them. And Advani was confident that the election would mark the end of the UPA.

Perhaps Singh felt the same. Certainly he knew he was on his way out. The best-case scenario for the Congress was that it would maintain its numerical strength in the Lok Sabha. If it did that then there was no way it could form a government on its own. It would have to go back to the Left. And the Left would not back Manmohan Singh. So, an informal understanding was reached. If the UPA got the numbers then the Congress would put forward Pranab Mukherjee as its prime ministerial candidate and the Left would back him.

Then, a miracle occurred. Once again the pollsters were wrong. The Congress actually won more seats than it did in 2004. Its tally went up from 145 to 206. It was now in such a strong position that it no longer needed the support of the Left.

Manmohan Singh had gambled—with the Congress' money, admittedly—and he had won. He made a triumphant return as prime minister.

Why did the UPA win in 2009. There are many theories but in essence it boils down to one of the two views. The first was the Congress party's view, that all the social sector schemes, the loan write-offs, the subsidies and the employment guarantee programmes had pleased the poor while the middle class had been pleased by the rapid economic growth during the UPA years. There is psephological evidence to back this view.

And then there was the view of Manmohan Singh himself. He believed it was his victory. The country had voted for his vision of India, his nuclear deal, his stewardship of the economy and his leadership. The man who had never won a municipal election in his life had now achieved the greatest feat of all. He had won a parliamentary election. As Sanjaya Baru said at the time, "Singh is King". And of course, you can marshal the psephological evidence to back this analysis as well.

* * *

So we'll never really know why the UPA won a second term. But some things are clear. The rapport that had existed between Sonia Gandhi and Manmohan Singh during UPA I had now broken down. People told Singh that as this was his own victory he should now act as though he was in charge. This is only a personal view but speaking as somebody who had known him for over two decades, I thought he became aloof, arrogant and complacent. You were either for him or against him. And if you were not completely for him, then he had no interest in you or your views. A little court of *chamchas* developed around the Prime Minister's Residence at 7, Race Course Road.

The contrary view is that he was still the same old Singh but felt an understandable frustration at Sonia Gandhi's refusal to let him act like a full-fledged prime minister. He was not allowed to choose his own ministers. Some

PMO appointments were subject to Sonia Gandhi's approval. And so on.

For all of UPA I, the government had managed to avoid giving the impression of two power centres. But now there were clearly two centres of power. The PMO did what it wanted. Some industrialists had a free run of the offices of senior officials. Men like Amar Singh became regular visitors. And the establishment became divided between Sonia's people and Manmohan's coterie.

Says Sanjaya Baru, 'My theory is that Manmohan Singh saw the 2009 victory as his. And I think he felt that this is now my government. But he was not allowed to function as if it was his government. Or he chose not to function... whatever: I can't get into the internal minds of individuals. When he found that he could not do what he wanted, he went into a shell. I wish at that point he had just quit. He could have quit without any controversy because he'd had a massive heart surgery in February 2009. But he chose to stay on and yet withdrew into a shell.'

This was a block of firewood waiting for a spark. And it came first with Singh's decision to be needlessly conciliatory to Pakistan in a meeting at the Egyptian resort of Sharm-el-Sheikh in July 2009. The Congress party attacked him. And when Sonia did not rush to his defence as she often had in the past, the troublemakers knew that the fire had started burning.

From this smouldering mess rose the ghosts of UPA I. The first was the Commonwealth Games scam. Everyone suspected that money was being made. Sports Minister Mani Shankar Aiyar even complained to Manmohan Singh. But the PM refused to listen.

Then, there was the 2G scam. Again, it had long been suspected that DMK ministers such as A Raja, the Telecom Minister, were less than straightforward in their dealings. But each time this was pointed out, the PM and Sonia Gandhi looked the other way. It was almost as though they believed that the UPA allies had a right to make money.

Next came the Coal Scam. This one really hurt because for part of the time when coal allotments had been made, Manmohan Singh himself was the Prime Minister and his signature appeared on many of the files.

The Congress now found itself answering questions from the Comptroller and Auditor General, an upright officer who had been appointed at P Chidambaram's urging, from the Supreme Court and from an increasingly hostile media.

Then the protests spread to the street. An anti-corruption movement masterminded by a former RTI activist called Arvind Kejriwal which used Anna Hazare as its figurehead, captured the public imagination. Then, a yoga practitioner called Baba Ramdev got into the act.

Throughout it all, the government had no strategy for dealing with the protests. It swung from one extreme to another. It dismissed Kejriwal one day and then sat down to parley with him on equal terms the next. Six ministers went to the airport to receive Baba Ramdev one day; his gathering was violently broken up by the police the following day.

Faced with this onslaught, the UPA funked it. Manmohan Singh went from smug arrogance following the 2009 victory to a state of paralysis. He stopped functioning as prime minister and nobody in the government, not his cabinet and not his bureaucrats took him seriously. Everyone simply did what they wanted.

Even the economy which had been part of the UPA I success story, stalled. Growth rates plummeted, inflation soared and under a new Finance Minister, Pranab Mukherjee—who also did not listen to Manmohan Singh—no liberalisation programmes went forward.

In 2009 Manmohan Singh had assured the country that with the Left gone, the reforms would go forward. He had promised untold benefits from the nuclear deal. He had bragged about India's closeness to America. He had lauded his own peace initiatives with Pakistan.

But nothing had worked. There were few reforms of consequence. The nuclear deal had yielded no visible benefit. India and America were actually further apart than they had been during Vajpayee's time. There was no improvement in relations with Pakistan.

Judged on every parameter that he had set out for himself in 2009, Manmohan Singh had been a disaster. After a wonderful first term, he had ended up being the worst prime minister in Indian history. He had gone from being a hero to educated Indians to becoming a figure of fun, and the butt of endless jokes. His own reputation for integrity had survived. But people asked: what good is it to have an honest Prime Minister if he lets everybody else make money?

Near the end of his term at a rare press conference, Manmohan was moved to pathetically declare that history would be kinder to him than contemporary opinion. Frankly, I doubt it. He will be remembered as the man who let India down.

As Sanjaya Baru says 'I think the UPA in the second term let down the country on every front: on foreign policy, on economic policy, on basic fiscal management of the economy. I think the government failed on a variety of fronts.'

Which leaves us with the mystery of Sonia Gandhi. She had come out of an intensely private existence to revive the Congress and to lead it to two election victories. Where was she when all this was happening? Where were her political instincts? Did she not see that the Congress was heading for disaster?

Nobody really knows the answers to these questions. The logical thing for her to have done was to have acceded to the party's demand to change the prime minister halfway through UPA II. Perhaps she was waiting for Manmohan to resign. But the same Manmohan Singh who had petulantly demanded that the party find him a majority for his nuclear deal, failing which he would resign, now determinedly clung to his chair. Even as his reputation sank lower and lower, he refused to even consider resigning.

Perhaps Sonia was waiting for her son Rahul Gandhi to be ready. But Rahul took too long to emerge and when he did, it was not clear if he was for the Manmohan Singh government or against it.

Worse still, he fought the worst election campaign in living memory. Having kept away from the press and having refused to tell us where he stood on major issues, he committed political harakiri in his first interview. After that, educated Indians simply stopped paying any attention to him. He was not helped by a dreadful DAVP style advertising campaign or by the directionless nature of the Congress's campaign.

Narendra Modi promised governance, jobs and a return to economic prosperity. Nobody has still worked out what it was that Rahul Gandhi was promising. By the time his mother and sister joined him on the campaign trail, it was too late. One exit poll revealed that over half of all voters made up their minds during the campaign. Had the Congress fought a better campaign, it might still have recovered some ground.

But when things go wrong, they go wrong absolutely. And so the UPA which began with a bang ended with another bang. Only this time, the bang was the sound of the explosion announcing Narendra Modi's arrival.